Honey – this looks
interesting, hope you
enjoy it.
Happy Valentines Day

Jack
2/14/78

The art of
making houses
liveable

Other Books by Peter Stevenson

The Art of Making Wooden Toys
The Greatest Days of Racing

The art of making houses liveable

by
Peter and Susanne Stevenson

photographs and illustrations by Peter Stevenson

Chilton Book Company Philadelphia New York London

Copyright © 1972 by Peter and Susanne Stevenson
First Edition   All Rights Reserved
Published in Philadelphia by Chilton Book Company
and simultaneously in Ontario, Canada,
by Thomas Nelson & Sons, Ltd.
Designed by Cypher Associates, Inc.
Manufactured in the United States of America

Library of Congress Cataloging in Publication Data

Stevenson, Peter, 1941-
  The art of making houses liveable.

  1. Dwellings—Remodeling. 2. Dwellings—Maintenance
and repair. 3. Interior decoration. I. Stevenson,
Susanne, 1940-   joint author. II. Title.
TH4816.S77   643'.7   72-8366
ISBN 0-8019-5698-6

For Shannon...

Acknowledgments

*All the photographs in this book were
taken of projects designed and built by
amateurs for their own homes.*

*Our thanks go to Joe and Joanie Laib,
John Garner, Sis and Doug Deeds, the Goods
and Bill Stevenson for entering into the
spirit of things and allowing us to photograph
some of their creations.*

*Our special thanks go to Phil Stanbro
for his much appreciated assistance.*

Contents

The art of
making houses
liveable

Introduction

About the book: When we first brought up the idea of writing a book on how to add new interest and value to an older house with a minimum of expense and building experience, the response was not overwhelmingly enthusiastic. It was much like announcing that we were planning to write a book about the Old South called *Gone With the Wind*.

Feet were shuffled, polite noises were made and embarrassment reigned until someone suggested helpfully, "Hasn't that been done before?"

"Ah," we said, spotting the area of confusion, "but ours is going to be different."

Ours (we went on to explain) will be written for the person who wants to do more to improve his surroundings than fix leaky faucets. Ours will be a book for those who don't like the idea of hiring decorators to tell them how to live— but who haven't had time to learn the tricks of defining their ideas and making them into tangible improvements. Ours, in short, will be exactly the kind of book we would have given anything for when we first entered this business of giving new life to old houses many years and half a dozen houses ago. As rewarding as the rebuilding of old houses can be, there are many pitfalls that the beginner could easily avoid if he only had the right kind of book: a book written with a keen appreciation of the amateur's point of view.

There are ways of getting things accomplished that are far better suited to an amateur builder (who would rather spend a little extra time to save a lot of extra money) than they are to a highly standardized professional. And there are professional techniques that should never be attempted by an amateur— no matter how simple they may appear on the printed page. On top of this, there are a host of interesting new products on the market which are opening up all sorts of exciting new possibilities to the amateur owner-builder. All these are to be the subject of our look at the art of creating a more imaginative place in which to spend our lives.

Our book will be different in other ways as well. For one thing, we'll never presume to dictate the latest set of decorating fads as though they were some

1

sort of gospel. In our opinion it makes more sense to discuss a few reliable tricks of the trade which we have found helpful in leading each person to define what *he* wants in *his own* house. What we'll be going into in some depth are ways to find out what worthwhile ideas are inside each of us and ways to turn these ideas into successful projects with a minimum of fuss and bother—and expense.

Why Bother?

Why should you spend any time adding to and changing the basic shell of your house, once the carpenter has finished with it?

Increased earning power from your real estate investment is one good reason to rebuild a house. The time and money spent to rebuild a house can come back to you many times over, whether from added borrowing power, resale or rental. The actual expense for raw materials is the lesser part of house building costs; and if you can do the jobs yourself, the results of a well-thought-out renovation can be amazingly rewarding and a fine way to invest any spare cash. There are even cases in which families have lived off the profits of rebuilding ripe old houses—although the repeated moving involved may not be everyone's cup of tea.

A growing family may be another good reason to take a good look at how you can get more out of your house. And a third reason to think about bringing an old, dull house to life is to enjoy the stimulus of living from day to

Here a variety of methods were used in concert to add a feeling of spaciousness to a cramped corner of a room. After a simple lean-to structure was added to a side yard, creating a new library area, the room was given still more depth by the use of mirrors.

2

day in more imaginative surroundings—where it's more fun to wake up than in the average cracker-box house.

If the animal psychologists are to be believed, "nesting," or building a nice place to spend the night, is one of those habits (that primates like gorillas and man have picked up over the eons) which fall into the category of Instinct Behavior (and we all know better than to mess around with instincts). Nesting is one of the few instincts we can indulge in as much as we like without gaining a lot of weight or running afoul of the law.

Psychologists tell us further that the kind of surroundings we allow ourselves to wander around in day after day may have more to do with the kind of moods and outlooks that become habitual than we might suspect. Whether the surroundings in which we spend a good proportion of our waking hours tend to lift our spirits a little each time we happen through them, or instead bring them down, can be increasingly important over the years.

Putting up new wallpaper in the bathroom may not make you one of the world's glamour people overnight. But then again, making a new place to live in can give you a new way of living—and it isn't going to hurt those spirits either. It can easily be one of the first tangible steps in the right direction.

Whatever the case, when a person finally decides that life is too short to miss having a house that's fun to live in, there are a number of different approaches he can take. He can look around for just the right house to fit his needs and moods. Or, if he's recently done well at the roulette tables, he can call in an architect and spell out just what he has in mind. But if he's like most of us, with details like jobs and limited time and limited funds to think about, he'll probably take the course most of us settle for: making the most of what he can find. And that is where this book comes in.

Using the Book as a Tool

Besides the obvious step-by-step hints for carrying out the various projects in each of the chapters, as well as the grids at the end of each chapter to help you plan each room in your house, we'll consider a number of more fundamental ideas about how to approach the whole challenge of giving new life to houses. We've found that these really work in practice. Without trying to wax too philosophic, we hope they will help you to define what you have in mind and to carry it off successfully in rebuilding your house rather than just patching it up.

There are a number of reasons why an amateur builder should usually try to rebuild rather than simply "patch up." The most basic reason lies in the way most houses are put together. Although the differences don't show much from the road, the modern house is a far cry from the product of the friendly, local old-style carpenter with his traditional pipe and his tried-and-true ways of building houses. For one thing, the economics have changed. Labor and financing costs run far higher than the expense of the actual materials used to build a house these days. To cut down on the size of the labor investment, scores of laborsaving products have come on the market in hope of finding favor with the Big Builders. The products are, of course, instantly grabbed up by the Little Builders as well, who also like to cut labor costs—and so we end up with much the same building techniques getting used in almost every house, no matter who builds it.

In his quest for bigger and better sales, the developer's goal is to offer the most lavish floor plan possible at the lowest price possible. To keep building costs within strict limits, he naturally specifies more and more laborsaving shortcuts as the price of labor skyrockets. As a result, the modern house has emerged a perfect example of what could be called one of the mixed blessings of the industrial age.

The average house is a collection of highly specialized arts like spray-textured ceilings and walls, laminated plastic veneer countertops and snapped-in aluminum window glazing. As such, the house can pose quite a problem to the homeowner when he decides it's time to do something about improving the place and would like to do some of the simple work himself to save the fantastic fees charged by specialized practitioners of the housing trades.

Do-it-yourself manuals have done their best to keep up with the new professional techniques, but more often than not, a special machine, together with a great deal of previous practice, is needed to get satisfactory results. When you're dealing with only one house in the first place, by the time you're just getting the hang of a technique, the job is all over—with most of it looking as if it was done by a beginner.

Many homeowners shy away from making obviously needed improvements in their own houses when they see the failures of other amateurs who have tried to imitate the highly practiced and specialized arts of the pros—and have gotten into more trouble than they could handle. But there is another way of going about it.

Few of us have the skills and equipment needed just to maintain the products of laborsaving devices. A hole burned in a laminated plastic counter is nearly impossible for a beginner to fix. Even a common doorknob hole in a plaster or gypsum-sheeting wall is tough to patch so that it doesn't make us cringe a little every time we see it.

As we've said, there's another way. Before trying to patch up an ailing wall or even a whole room, it might be a good idea to step back and take a look at the basic goals of your projects before warming up the tools. For instance, if it's a question of doctoring a gypsum-board or plaster wall that has a few holes, stop and think about the whole problem before buying the patching plaster.

Did you really like the wall when it was in one, unscarred piece? Is it really worthwhile to work like the devil just to re-create a wall texture that wasn't exactly thrilling to begin with? Or would you do better to look around for more imaginative ways to cover the wall?

Bear in mind that most techniques rely on machinelike uniformity as a standard of excellence. The only way a professional can judge his work is by the overall flatness of his plaster wall or by the perfect straight edge of his countertop—regardless of whether or not a featureless, flat surface or razor-edge straightness is appealing.

Right now, all over the country, builders are diligently perfecting flat surfaces and straight edges only to retire in later years to Mexico or Hawaii or Europe, where they can enjoy the easygoing and appealing rough textures and crooked edges of the buildings of the countryside.

So, before lifting a hammer, take a close look at the alternatives. You can try your best to perfect a specialized technique in one afternoon, and if you're a genius with a trowel you may get lucky and re-create the same old cracker-box wall you started with. Or you can call a pro in on the job, spend a bit of cash and end up with a perfectly restored cracker-box wall.

On the other hand, you can face the problem head-on and look around for a more interesting way to cover the wall with a surface that will be easier to cope with and usually more durable than the original. And by putting your money solely into materials to make your house more appealing and easier to maintain instead of paying off someone else's labor and overhead, you start to get a real return from the money invested in your real estate.

There's another reason why a homeowner should usually try to rebuild rather than patch up—a morale reason. It's nearly impossible, even for a well-seasoned pro, to patch something without the patch job's showing through. The paint doesn't dry quite the same on the new surface as it did on the surrounding wall, or the texture is slightly different. Something always seems to make even a competent patch-up job show a little; and every time you notice this, you're reminded once again that the old place is slowly getting older and more patchy-looking all the time.

If, instead of just trying to hold the line with mending jobs, you attack the wear-and-tear problem with projects that rebuild the house with innovative materials (even if it's done just a little at a time), then the house begins to take on a new mood of regeneration. It can become almost like a live thing, constantly regrowing and providing new opportunities for expressing what you like best.

Even the old, shredded areas of the house can lose their power to depress when you know that new life is growing, however slowly, through the old place. In fact, some of the most enjoyable houses we've seen have never quite reached that static "finished" state from which most houses start to decline. It seems as if some of the most stimulating houses are constantly kept alive with new growth and, in turn, help keep their inhabitants alive by providing an exciting place to roam around in.

The process of finding and making use of new ways to add interest to a drab or worn out house is like any other enterprise in many ways. There are all sorts of helpful tricks of the trade and work secrets—as well as a host of pitfalls to be avoided along the way. After spending a number of years falling into nearly every pit we could find, we've finally come to realize a few trial-and-error truths about dealing with houses.

In arranging these ideas into a book, the scheme is to present a layout that

In studio rooms imagination can be a better key to success than a fat budget. Here simple board shelves and a trunk-table are arranged to create an inviting corner at a minimum outlay. Scraps of colored glass set into a wooden frame serve to cover up a metal window frame.

will make the ideas you're looking for at the moment easy to find and not buried under things that won't become important until you reach another point in your housebuilding plans. Of course, each reader will probably want to start the regeneration process at a different point in the house, and so the book has been arranged with flexibility in mind in the hope of providing a useful tool to make the job easier, cheaper and more satisfying.

In the first section of the book you'll find general topics—the kind of challenges common to every house, such as gathering ideas you like, defining these ideas and checking them against what is actually possible in your house. General work methods that make all jobs easier to start as well as finish will be discussed.

Then, in the separate chapters to follow you'll find a discussion of specific problems and opportunities that we usually run into in each of the different rooms of a house: the living room, kitchen, bathroom, and so forth. After each of the alternatives available to you in every room has been described, there follows a third section containing the separate, specific, step-by-step instructions for carrying out any of the alternatives you decide to use in your own house.

In the second section we progress room by room through the house for several reasons. First of all, the process of rebuilding an older house is a proposition entirely different from building a whole new structure. In building a new house the contractor progresses task by task through the most efficient sequence of steps to raise a house—from digging the foundation ditches to laying the drains to pouring the slab. Each different craftsman shows up on the site for only the time needed to progress to the next step in the sequence.

But in rebuilding a house, especially one that is being lived in at the time, it's an entirely different process. Instead of ripping into the whole house at one time (which is admittedly the most efficient way), the home rebuilder is obviously better off starting with a single room project and moving at his own speed through the house without having the whole place in an uproar. It's easier on the budget to do a little at a time; and it's sometimes easier to get ideas by starting with the part of the house where you know what changes you want, letting the new look of the house then spread easily and naturally through the rest of the rooms.

Last but not least, the easiest way to get started on the whole house is to begin with that one outstanding project that has been on your mind for some time—whether it's an eyesore that has been bothering you all along or just an obvious sort of project that looks easy and rewarding to carry out.

Old boatbuilders will tell you that the hardest part of building a boat is making that first cut. The same goes for houses. It's sometimes pretty difficult to get up nerve to rip into a room and get a project under way—no matter how easy the job proves to be later on. Even after years of building, all of us occasionally fall into that mood of not believing that we can do *anything* to improve things until we force ourselves to jump in with both feet, give it a try and find out just how easy and rewarding it is to deal with houses.

Houses are pretty simple things compared to boats, planes, cars and many other works of man that play a part in our daily life. Once a few basic rules have been laid down, they're easy to deal with—if you don't listen to those who like to embellish their crafts with mysterious-sounding jargons.

Another reason to separate one section of the book according to room use is that the techniques and alternatives can vary greatly depending on the function of the room. What makes good flooring sense in the bedroom may be completely wrong for a family playroom. What is good painting practice in the living room is taboo in the kitchen. So, instead of hiding the kitchen-painting technique among all the other painting methods, we've included it with the wall covering alternatives available to you for kitchen use. This way you can compare side by side the effects, durability and amount of work involved for all the choices open to you in the kitchen.

In each chapter you'll find a number of aids to help you take stock of what you already have as a given set of conditions. It's important to have a clear picture of what you have to work with before you start to think about which alternative design ideas will work and which may be impossible in your particular case. The more clearly you can define the limits you have to work within, the easier it is to come up with workable rebuilding schemes for your own house.

To help out in this cause, we've included a type of floor- and wall-plan grid layout that we've found indispensable to coming up with new, or at least usable, ideas. The grids are divided into squares, representing one foot each, so you can pace off the existing floor plan of a room on the grid. Once you have a picture of the room, then the choice among your alternatives (such as room dividers, wall component shelves, built-ins and fixture positioning) becomes more evident. By using the design layout grids you can easily test to see whether a certain inspiration will work in actual practice.

In the bathroom and kitchen sections you'll find scale patterns of fixtures such as sinks and bathtubs, and so forth, which can be cut out and used to show the existing layout of your room (or to help the creative juices to flow in planning possible new layouts).

After you've found out what is already there, you can move on to comparing the various alternative plans, building methods and materials as well as ways to work in your own new ideas. Once you're acquainted with the choices open to you, you can make a sensible plan to fit your design goals into your budget and building capability.

Examing the Status Quo

The goal of the book is to provide an incentive to carry out those simple modifications that can add the human touch and feel of quality to the bare shell left by the builder. At times, in our exasperation with the frailties and lack of character of some forms of modern housing, we may grow critical of expedient modern building methods. (Who, after all, can argue that covering a wall with a thin cardboard-and-gypsum sandwich is a durable or even an attractive solution? Yet the vast majority of houses are walled with either this strange concoction or lath and plaster—neither of which is exactly bullet-proof.)

Wall components can be free-standing as well as built-in. This small edition can be moved to suit the furniture arrangement.

But there is another side of the coin to be reckoned with. It has to be admitted that the results of typical mass-production building methods *are* usually reasonably weathertight and sturdy enough for most occasions. If such a house somehow just misses conveying the idea that it was made by loving hands just for you, there's no need to reach for gasoline-soaked rags and a match. It's a rare house that's beyond all hope of salvation; and in most cases it's these very laborsaving, drab, unimaginative building methods throughout a house which allow a builder to provide a floor plan that we would have been unable to afford otherwise.

Thanks to these laborsaving methods, we have all the delights of more and greater washers, dryers, disposals, toilets and telephones. True, we may pay for these luxuries by waking every day to monotonous cracker-box walls shot from guns, lifeless extruded window frames and featureless spray-on glitter textures. But these we can deal with: A wall can be given an imaginative, durable covering in a few hours and for surprisingly little outlay. It's pretty tough, though, to put in the extra toilet that would be missing if the cost-saving methods weren't used when the house was first built for sale. So we may have come out well in the bargain after all.

Whatever the case, the fact remains that unless you yourself dictate the look and shape of the surroundings in which you spend a good many of your waking hours, someone else will—by default. In a world where so much of life comes to us preprogrammed, prepackaged and predigested, it seems a bit of a loss to miss out on the fun of creating your own stimulating living center that reflects all the things in life that you happen to enjoy.

Whether you're looking for the satisfaction of watching a dull, time-worn house take on new life and personality or just looking for a way to get the most from your investment dollar, we hope that this book will help make it easier to find both.

1

Getting Started
With New Ideas

Finding a way to inject a little imagination and interest into a lifeless house is a challenge. It can be attacked the same way you'd approach any of the knottier of life's dilemmas, whether it's solving the Sunday crossword or developing a new theory of physics. First you define your "knowns" and then you use these to help work out the "unknowns." Any Sherlock Holmes fan will tell you that.

Getting under way is often simply a task of clarifying those vague notions you may have about a mood or a "look" you'd like to work into a room. Of course, if your mind is as blank as Modred's shield and you haven't the foggiest idea what to do with the place, then the job is a little more difficult. But more often than not, people have more definite ideas about what they want than they may realize. Defining what you have to work with can often bring these ideas out into the open. While you're noting the features of the existing house as a starting point, you may want to jot down those parts which you wouldn't mind keeping as they are. As we said earlier, it's a rare house that is so thoroughly repellent as to defy salvage, and there are almost always a few features and rooms that may suit your purposes with only minor changes—or none at all.

Note those features of the house which you know you are dissatisfied with (and probably already have a good idea how to remedy). Those parts of the house that are not too bad as is and those parts which are definite eyesores with obvious solutions can be thought of as the "knowns" of the house. The remainder of the house—those areas which are vaguely unsatisfying but which present no easily recognized remedies—we can call the "unknowns." It's these last parts that will test our design genius.

If a good proportion of the house happens to fall within the "knowns," then you may be able to work out a Master Plan which can sometimes make it easier to fill in the blank spaces with ideas derived from the surrounding projects.

However, if much of the house seems to fall in the region of the Great Unknown, then it's often a waste of time struggling to come up with a Master

Plan in a single sitting. It's usually a better idea in this event to choose a specific project somewhere in the house that you *do* have definite ideas about, and then complete this to your liking. Once the completed project can be viewed in the flesh, it will often spawn new ideas for adjoining areas, and the new look can spread through the house gradually, creating new ideas as it goes.

The only advantage of a Master Plan is that if you can decide ahead of time that several rooms will have the same paint or carpeting, for instance, then you can sometimes find a bargain by buying in quantity.

If there is one particular eyesore that bothers you about the house, then getting under way may not pose much of a problem. But if there are several areas that suggest themselves as starting points, it may be a good idea to start off with the job that seems to pose the least challenge to your pocketbook as well as your building skills, yet which promises good visual rewards for your trouble. It's important to get the house off to a good start, and it may be a smart idea to begin with something fairly simple to get your feet wet. If you haven't been doing handwork for a while, start with an easy and satisfying job just to get a little success under your belt and taste the rewards of your efforts.

If, however, after reading over the suggested alternative materials and methods you still feel that you don't have enough definite ideas to get under way, there are various tricks to help build clearer ideas of which projects would create the effects you want.

If you don't have any better ideas but want to get going, start out with a simple room (not a bathroom or a kitchen, which presents lots of complicated possibilities) that seems to be especially unsatisfying, no matter how vague the room's drawbacks may be to you. Then use the old "knowns to unknowns" method that we used on the whole house to help clarify what can be done to help this particular area. List the room's features which don't seem to require change, then list the definite eyesores, and finally try some of the alternatives suggested in the related room section, either on the floor-plan grid provided in the chapter or by using simple mock-ups to approximate the effect of each, to see which one you like best in real life. This is where the rebuilder of a house has a great advantage over an architect. The original designer of the house must use what skills and talents he has to make an educated guess as to what will actually look attractive in a house when his drawings are re-created in full-scale and three dimensions.

The rebuilder, however, has an already existing, three-dimensional volume to work with. If a room seems too large and barnlike for some intangible reason, he can simply put up divider walls or built-ins to correct the error that didn't show up on the original floor plan. If the room seems too small, he can resort to mirrors or additional window area or a number of other visual tricks to adjust for an existing mistake. If a certain window has particularly good lighting and a nice view, then the rebuilder can work to emphasize this window to draw attention away from the drawbacks of the room. More often than not, house plans pay absolutely no attention to natural lighting at dif-

12

ferent times of day or to the surrounding views, so the original designer is usually unable to visualize the effects that these surroundings have on a house.

Large window areas tend to be placed according to the outside appearance of the house rather than to the view they provide. With so many middlemen coming between the designer of the house and the builder of the actual structure, it isn't unusual to see huge windows facing out toward nothing, whereas a perfectly good view off to one side may go completely unnoticed. The amateur rebuilder can do much to increase the attractiveness of his house simply by correcting the mistakes created by a system that forces the average architect to design a house without regard to the location and without the time to fix obvious errors once the house is built.

Cardboard or a spare sheet of paneling can help when testing out remedies for an unimaginative room. You can cover windows or doors to test changes of the existing walls. Just prop up the covering temporarily, then stand back and see how you like the effect. The paneling can be used to simulate a room divider wall to test ways of breaking up the volume of a boxlike room into more usable and more interesting smaller areas.

As hard as it is to believe at times, experience has shown that divider walls can actually make a room seem to contain more usable space, despite the fact that they obviously take up floor area. This is evident if you've ever watched a house being built. When the floor plan is laid out, it seems impossible that anyone could live in such a tiny area; but once the walls are up to give volume to the floor area, the living space begins to look much larger. If you could somehow scoop out all the interior walls of a typical house, the resulting shell would look hardly larger than a small garage. If you don't believe it, climb up on the roof and see how tiny the overall floor plan of your own house suddenly looks.

If divider walls can make the volume of a house seem larger, the same is true, to a degree, in a larger room, which may need more interesting areas to create a cozier setting and a more versatile room. To test the theory, have a helper stand a sheet of plywood or paneling in various positions to see whether you want to split up the room and, if so, to determine exactly where the divider wall should be.

Paneling with a dark grain can also serve as a rough approximation of a darker shade of wall paint, and the lighter reverse side can show what sort of effect a lighter hue will create on a wall.

When you stand a dark panel against the wall, you'll notice that the wall seems to come closer to you, whereas a lighter shade will make the wall appear farther away. So, if a room is too large and barnlike, or if an end wall looks too remote, you might try a darker shade of paneling or paint to create an illusion which will remedy the fault.

The same sort of thing is true for ceilings. If a ceiling seems too high, try a darker color to make it seem closer to you.

So, whether you use cardboard boxes to simulate built-in furniture or

13

Arches work equally well, whether painted or stained, to relieve the square, boxy lines found around shelves and doors.

shelves, or sheets of paneling to mock up dividers, try any method you can think of to test your ideas. Simulations will not only prevent mistakes in design but they'll also lead you to many new ideas, simply because they make it so easy to try a wide variation of guesses in the actual setting.

Getting Inspirations

One of the best ways we've found of getting inspirations is to start collecting examples (photos or magazine clippings) of other people's work that happen to capture a mood you like. This process works wonders in several different ways. If you're actively on the lookout for good ideas, your eyes will slowly become accustomed to seeing more and more than they used to, as you make your rounds during the day. And when you become aware of the challenges in creating pleasant surroundings, you'll begin to build up your own strong beliefs and tastes that can solve many design dilemmas.

It doesn't really make any difference where you find the ideas—in a housing magazine or in the background behind the models in a fashion magazine or in the latest issue of a magazine at the local barbershop. If it conveys some sort of mood or possibly a construction detail that could add authenticity to decorative style, rip it out and save it with the rest.

There's a funny thing about lifting other people's ideas—it's one of the best ways of coming up with original ideas of your own. Someone once said about gypsy guitarists that the reason they all have such individual styles is that they're all trying to do exactly the same thing. No matter how closely you try to follow someone else's brainstorm, by the time you get through translating the theme into materials that you can cope with and dimensions that fit your particular situation, the project usually becomes so encrusted with your own little preferences and last-minute inspirations that the designer of the original idea would have a hard time recognizing his influence.

A scrapbook (or a scrapbox) of housing ideas is also a great place to store all those folders they give away at lumber and supply yards advertising new building products and shades of paint. It is, as well, a place to keep the names and addresses of bargain building material suppliers and interesting junk shops that you encounter in your travels.

Wherever you find a picture of a housing idea that you like (whether you happen to be working on a related project or not), grab it and stuff it in the scrapbook for future reference. Even if the idea is a lavish treatment of a château in the wine country or a loft in Rome, if you like it and it conveys some sort of feeling to you, save it. You'll probably run across some new material or construction breakthrough at a later date that will permit you to re-create the mood in your own house.

As the scrapbook gets fatter and fatter, you'll begin to notice that the process of coming up with "original" ideas will start to come easier to you.

A word of caution may be in order when using ideas found in housing magazines. The editors and staffs of these magazines are constantly under the pressure of a deadline and must regularly come up with more decorative inspirations in a single year than most of us have to deal with in a lifetime. Everyone has occasional flat spots, and as the deadline hysteria slowly builds to a fever pitch, some very strange ideas can begin to look pretty good to an editor under stress. Almost any project will look good and make a nice page layout after a professional graphic artist and an imaginative photographer get through with it; but some of them are not quite so easy to carry off in real life as others.

The key to whether a project which looks good in a do-it-yourself article is really workable or not lies in the word "availability." If you have available both the same degree of talent and exactly the same shades and textures of materials as the ones used in the article, then you stand a chance of bringing off the same effect seen in the magazine. But beware the fancy photographer

A wastebasket has been set into the top of this counter bench to get it out of the way (and allow easier bank shots). The picture frame on the wall folds down...

...to form an added work table, and the work bench can then be used as a seat for the table.

with fisheye lenses that distort and lights that dramatize, for tricky photography is often a handy cover-up for an idea that is basically ugly when the project is seen in the cold hard light of morning.

Also beware of highly professional graphics used to carry off an idea in a project. Bold, impressive supergraphic stick-ons may look great when executed by a well-equipped graphic artist with access to all sorts of beautiful special color supplies and years of experience in fine finish detail. The same project when done by an average amateur, working with the limited art supplies normally available, and viewed after several months of everyday wear and tear of kids and pets, can look somewhat different from the original concept.

Some of the projects which fall into this category are the type that depend on the new superglues for their structural integrity. These catalyzed glues are amazing in their ability to make foreign objects stick together, but the types on the market for public consumption are usually highly inflexible. After the repeated expansion and contraction of the various stuck-together parts in getting hot and cold in the normal course of things, they seem to work their way loose and eventually pop apart with disconcerting ease.

If the appeal of a project depends largely on a special combination of color shades, bear in mind that professionals who do nothing but set up projects for page layouts have a much wider range of hues available to them than you can find in a durable paint at an average home supply store. If colors are important, check to see what shades are actually at your disposal before buying the rest of the materials for the project.

Just remember that if a certain design style depends on clean, crisp, exact finish and bright, unblemished surfaces, textures and colors for its appeal, then you're going to have to maintain it in top shape to retain the attractiveness of your work.

Design Styles

This is where historic or period design themes have the advantage. Some of the old design styles come to us already rough-hewn and worn around the edges. The rougher and more weather-beaten they get, the better they can look—which is no little boon to the person who hates constant maintenance.

A rough-hewn style, whether it's Tudor, Spanish, Alpine or Polynesian, tends to blend into nature gracefully over the years of wear and tear and only looks mellower and more attractive the older it gets. On the other hand, the house design styles that must stand out in crisp contrast to the surrounding colors of nature often need constant attention to keep their shiny, well-manicured appeal.

We're not trying to sell either type of design style, but the point is that it may be a good idea to examine the styles you might like to use in your house in view of the kind of work you like to do.

Some people find it relaxing to putter around the house occasionally, keeping things up to standard, whereas others find fun only in creating new things and can't stand to waste time maintaining what's already there. Of course, choosing a rough or a fine finish style doesn't automatically lock you into a certain period of history. In the modern vein there are crisp, clean futuristic motifs as well as the very rustic contemporary look. There are clean, well-manicured historic designs like the Colonial or Ante Bellum plantation look, and then there are the rougher old styles such as Spanish or Mediterranean.

Naturally, what each of us defines as a comfortable, friendly and inviting house, reflecting the mood of living we find attractive, will vary widely from one person to the next. The array of styles that greets us in a furniture showroom can be pretty bewildering at times, with Japanese, Danish, 1930's Futuristic, Colonial, Victorian-Nostalgic and all the others jammed together in one room. But most of us have already formed tastes that narrow the choice to just a few styles that seem to ring a bell. In the case of the house itself, after testing each of our favorites in the light of its upkeep demands and the difficulty of construction, we can usually narrow the field of choice still further.

In Europe, where there are often strict rules governing the outside appearance of buildings to present an attractive appearance in the whole community, people have become used to finding interior designs that contrast greatly with the outside of the building. Staid old edifices are often filled with wild, futuristic interiors, and the whole arrangement seems to work out nicely.

The same situation is true to a degree in a community of mass-built housing. There really isn't much you can do to erase the look of a house built with mass-production techniques on the outside. Some give it a halfhearted try with a nostalgic form of gingerbreading in an attempt to recapture the individual charm of days gone by, but the results are generally pretty laughable. Modern houses have a proportion all their own, and to stick on a few hopeful Japanese or Polynesian trim details or a bit of Victorian scrollwork doesn't fool anybody. Inside, however, the story is different—you have more control over the entire field of view. There's nothing to say you can't create any kind of surrounding that hits your fancy.

In fact, in creating a mood for the surroundings of our home we seem to have more freedom of choice than in any other field of social endeavor. You might feel a little silly running to the market dressed in the style of the time of Louis XIV, but no one bats an eyelash if you spend a great deal of money furnishing your whole house in the chairs and tables and whatnot of that very same period.

Few of us travel around dressed in Tahitian lavalavas, yet the sight of a room filled with Polynesian rattan furniture doesn't exactly cause the jaw to drop in astonishment, even in Idaho. People who are often keenly alive to the slightest deviation from the norm in the kind of car they drive or the style of dress worn are completely conditioned to finding all manner of furnishing and housing styles that are out of context.

We live in an age of romanticism, in which anywhere but here and anytime but now seem to find favor the world over. Nightclubs in Paris are named for beaches in Tahiti and bars in Tahiti are called after famous spots in Paris. The only rule seems to be: Anything goes.

The point of all this is that there is really no one you can look to for direction but yourself—even if you wanted to. So the task at hand is to figure out what sort of house pleases you most—if you don't already have a good idea.

Of course, depending on your tastes, you may not want to follow any previous design style but rather come up with an original look that you like. Whatever your preferences, a well-stocked scrapbook can be of immeasurable help when deciding on a design direction for your house, even if you choose to take a little from this style and a few things from that motif.

If you're like the rest of us, you'll probably find that the styles that appeal to you are often linked to a way of life that appeals to you. So, if you're at a bit of a loss for a place to start making your design decisions, you might try coming at it from the rear. What sort of life appeals to you in your leisure time? If you'd like to follow a certain sport or live in a certain corner of the world, or if you find that a certain period of history arouses some strange enthusiasm in you, why not let this interest become part of your surroundings? Why not bring it out into the open where it may be able to remind you of the more exciting aspects of living during the day-to-day grind?

The reason we stress themes to hang a house design style on is that in order to get a positive response from you, a design theme has to stand for something or to represent a certain train of thought. Any house will remind you of something, whether you want it to or not—even if it recalls just a motel room in East Wagon Wheel, Utah. So long as we're stuck with the fact that everything reminds us of something we've seen before, we might as well have it remind us of something we like.

Once you have a theme, you'll find many design ideas suddenly growing out of the theme itself and suggesting themselves. Restaurant designers know how well this approach works, for they are keenly alive to any trick that will create a surrounding that is fun just to be in, and one which you'll want to return to. Attractive restaurants nearly always have strong central themes which are followed boldly with the same lack of restraint that would make a house more fun to live in.

The first objection most people have to strong central themes is that they fear they will be hard to live with over an extended period. What might be fun to visit occasionally at a restaurant, for example, may not wear well over years of use. However, we've found that the opposite is actually the effect of long periods spent with a strong central theme. Instead of growing tiresome, the emphasis of a motif tends to fade a little as you become adapted to it and you can almost become "hooked" on having a richer and richer visual surrounding.

Another criticism of strong central themes is that they can create a nasty case of "culture shock" when one is traveling from room to room. This was certainly true in those nineteenth century Romantic houses in which a rich

19

dowager allowed her enthusiasm for interior decorators to run amok. Just walking from the Rococo "Blue Room" to the "Oriental Room" was enough to make your eyes water. But we've found that when a homeowner rebuilds his house, a certain individual style of execution is evident throughout, giving a nice feeling of continuity to the whole effort—no matter what varied themes have been indulged in within the different rooms.

Junk as a Source of Inspiration

"Junking," the going on expeditions to find all manner of interesting bits of junk and antiques, is one of the fascinating little tasks that can help make the rebuilding of a house more fun; and it can be started at any time regardless of your rebuilding schedule. By "junk," of course, we mean any sort of useless or semiuseless piece of memorabilia that you happen to like.

If the "antique" is part of your family and its heritage, all the better (provided you like your heritage, of course). Just about any piece, worthless or not, that gets a positive response from you can form the focal point for building the mood of a whole room. The only type of junk that should be avoided is the type that may be all the rage at the moment but which doesn't really touch a nerve in you—no matter how much it might bring at a hock shop. Expensive silver or a carrousel horse that has no meaning to you, outside of the fact that everybody else seems to want it, can be a total waste of money.

There is usually an amazing array of folk art in most families' junk boxes stored away somewhere—little pieces of your life that would look surprisingly intriguing when properly displayed and lighted. Better by far to have your first skate key in a glass case than to go without fresh meat just to buy a highly pedigreed but meaningless antique.

Nothing is quite so sad as the fabulously expensive, richly decorated house in which every last piece of furniture, bric-a-brac and curiosity has been bought from catalogues. Personality is something that simply doesn't have a price tag on it, and despite the lavish budgets poured into these houses to insure that the place will have a ready-made "lived in" feeling of heritage, the result is seldom more appealing than a furniture showroom.

We've all seen examples of this sort of thing, and it simply goes to point up that drabness and sterile dullness aren't limited to economy housing. The appeal of a house isn't a direct function of the thickness of the wallet; surprisingly inviting houses can be built, or rebuilt, for very little cost per square foot if you use good judgment.

Shopping for junk is somewhat different from shopping for bargain building materials, as we'll see farther on. One of the marks of an experienced junk shopper is profound patience and coolness under fire. If you find a piece that particularly intrigues you, but you can't quite go the price, it's best to make a polite offer of what you would pay for it—and when it's turned down, wait until you run across another one. That unique little antique you want so badly often has a way of turning up in much the same form in a different shop later on, usually at a more attractive price.

Just as an example of how this can work, we once found in a shop two pieces that we suddenly found we desperately needed. Piece A was priced well above our range of operations, whereas Piece B had a price tag that was more reasonable. So we grabbed B and regretfully left A to its fate. A little later in another shop we found a piece almost identical to A, as well as one that could have been B's double. This time, however, the prices were reversed, with A reasonable and B with a highly optimistic price tag. The moral of the story is, of course, to make every effort to avoid that silly feeling you get when you know you're paying too much for something. If the price is too high, step back and wait awhile for another one. Like women and streetcars, there'll be another one along in a little while (although, come to think of it, we haven't seen a streetcar for years).

Factum, Non Verbae

We now come to a point in the discussion which may well prove to be old stuff to those who are familiar with the workings of the creative process. But a word or two on the subject might make things easier for those who find dealing with the arts, even the art of creating an attractive house, to be a new experience.

One of the first and most important rules for performing the trick of pulling ideas out of yourself and making them into something tangible is: Listen to yourself and take the advice of others (even us) with a grain of salt.

This is, as you've probably already noticed, actually two rules, but they seem to go together all the time, and they're equally important to knocking down the barriers to creativity. The first part is sometimes the harder to follow of the two.

From time to time we all seem to get wild brainstorms and crazy hunches that we can't help feeling would work out well in actual practice, no matter how ridiculous they may sound when we try to describe them to the next-door neighbor. In a case such as this, we've found that it's best just to go ahead with the project without telling anybody, friend or family, about it. It will work out better for everybody.

If you go around broadcasting your brainstorms, one of two things will happen: Everyone will call you a genius for having thought of it and you will suddenly find you no longer have such a burning desire to build the project because you've already gotten your reward; or everybody will make you feel like a fool for having thought of it and you'll forget the whole idea, no matter how well it might have worked out in actual practice. So, mum's the word. Talking only dissipates action. Besides, if the brainstorm begins to look like a loser about halfway through, you can always clean things up in a jiffy and say you were just testing your tools or something.

In most cases it's very important to give your projects a real chance to shine when the housebuilding muses have seared your brain with sudden ambition.

Act fast when you feel a brainstorm coming, for on second thought you may well "chicken out" of building a really innovative idea when the initial enthusiasm begins to ebb. Try to resist wanting to rip the whole thing out when it's only half completed. Things generally look pretty grim when you get about halfway through; you're beginning to tire of the idea and you may have run into a little trouble by then. In their unfinished form, most projects fall quite a bit below the stirring effect you had pictured in your mind. But stick it out, and nine times out of ten, things will come out the way you want them to in the end.

For some reason we've found most people are a little hesitant to try out their own ideas even when they're truly clever and original innovations. It always

Faced with the drabness of just-another-typical-square-door, this builder ripped out the old and replaced it with a paneled door built up from old packing crate lumber. The arched door opening was created by cutting two arched fillers from 1" stock to fit in the top of the door frame. The curved surface of the arch frame is made from 1/8" plywood set into rabbeted notches in the 1" stock.

Through the arched opening are more doors which have carried out the arch theme with a simpler modification: an easy-to-make arched header board with routed designs.

seems that the projects we are most uncertain of, because they are untested by public response, are the very ones that get the most heartwarming reception when viewed by the world. When you follow your innermost building urges, you usually find (to your unending surprise) that others tend to like those urges even better than the projects you got as secondhand inspiration.

Most of us have little difficulty in taking advice with a grain of salt when we know we're on solid ground and are sure of our facts. But when people start flowing with all sorts of helpful hints on what you should do with your house, the shrewd rebuilder realizes that even if the helper knows what he's talking about, there is no greater expert on what you really like than yourself. In that field, at least, you can't be approached.

Free advice can be helpful, however, in a roundabout way. When the fatherly flow of handy hints begins, keep a close watch on your own reactions to the advice; you may often pick up new ideas that will make the project even better. Constructive criticism has a way of stirring up the creative juices to make your brainstorms more impressive.

Professional advice is almost always negative. Suggest the simplest modification of mass-production techniques to a professional man and he'll tell you it's impossible. This is mostly the result of the fact that he has learned the hard way that oddball approaches and solutions simply don't pay off when you have to make a profit to stay alive. The pros rely on predictable techniques that can be depended on to make money. When they get into something offbeat, they can easily spend so much time getting used to a new approach that their profits go down the drain. So they've learned that the only way to keep eating regularly is to say that anything out of the ordinary is impossible, even when the unorthodox approach might make sense for the homebuilder.

Caveat Emptor

Sometimes even folders describing building materials put out by the manufacturers aren't much more reliable than the other forms of free advice. We've seen some materials described as unsuitable for use in bathrooms withstand tough conditions over a period of long usage *in* a bathroom better than similar materials specifically made for use in that room. So when it comes right down to it, your guess is just about as good as anybody's. Keep your eyes open, carefully examine the materials you buy before leaving the store, and use your own good judgment as to what will work and what won't.

It's sometimes disconcerting when you run across a situation in which you are forced to realize that the experts may not know much more than you do about a subject (and you *know* you don't know much). But it happens more often than we'd like to admit, and the only thing we can count on is good old common sense.

The natural impulse when reading a paint-can label that says "Black" is to surmise that the can is filled with black paint—and all's right with the world. But if you deal with packaged materials for any length of time, you'll begin to

23

realize that labels are often just hopeful guesses. "Black" simply means that the chances are in your favor that the paint inside the can is black. But if you don't have a lot of time to waste making trips back and forth to the store to get the color you want, always have the can opened and check the hue just to make sure. We used to drive mile on unnecessary mile before we finally overcame the natural diffidence of a consumer and started asking to have the cans opened before taking off with the wrong paint but the right label. New clerks will look at you as if you've been whiffing the paint fumes too long, but the veterans will understand and your gas bill will diminish visibly. This goes for all packaged goods, including sealed spray cans. If the color is what it says it is, you'll buy. If not, you'll be back anyway, so they might as well break the seal and test it.

When buying lumber it's always a good idea to take a stroll out to the actual pile of wood while the man chooses your boards. It's simply a polite way of telling him that you appreciate good lumber enough to make a special effort; and he'll usually respond by pulling the best boards for you. If you show him that you don't care about what you get, he'll save the good ones for someone who does.

Built-ins don't have to be anchored to the framework to qualify as such. This end table is a simple box covered with tongue-and-groove lumber, a bit of paneling on the top and a few pieces of ornate hardware.

24

If it's important to the project to have nice-looking grain, it might be worthwhile to help load the boards so you can get a closer look at the grain, the straightness and the dryness of the boards without insulting anybody. Roll each board onto its side edge and sight down this edge. If the board bows a little to one side or the other, it's not too serious; but if the board arches over the top or sags in the middle when held on edge, it's better to change it for another—it'll be absolutely useless to you and will cause all sorts of problems if you try to use it.

If a particular board seems much heavier than the others of like size, then it's still wet and hasn't been cured enough. This makes the board easy to nail, hard to saw and may well mean that it will split when nailed into place and left to dry, and then will shrink. So it's usually a good idea to stay clear of the heavy ones—"the ones with the birds' nests still in them," as the lumbermen call them.

Swirling, dramatic grain patterns are great for decoration. However, if it's strength you're after, stick to the boards with straight grains. Keeping in mind the way the boards will be used will help you to get enough attractive ones for the project without putting too much strain on the lumberyard's supplies. In most projects some of the boards just won't show, and it's a bit of a waste to hide a nice board away in a corner if the next customer could use it better.

Most lumberyards carry a variety of grades of lumber, and generally you pay for what you get. The grades vary all the way from "A-Clear" (nicely finished with no knots) down to "Shop Grade" (looks as if the mice have been at it). A relatively inexpensive all-around grade for framing is "Construction Grade."

If you need a special piece of wood for a project that demands an extra-nice finish or a special stock, this can be found at a hardwood specialty yard, where you can also find special sizes of all woods.

Plywood, as everybody knows, comes in a variety of thicknesses, grades and even sheet sizes. Most local yards carry 1/4, 3/8, 1/2, 5/8, 3/4 and possibly 1 inch thicknesses. The sheets come in either interior or exterior grade, which has to do with the type of glue used. Exterior is made with waterproof glue and can be used outside or near steam and water without coming apart. Not so with the interior grade, which does not stand up well near any trace of water for any length of time, but then it's cheaper and may be just what you need for temporary use.

There are also various quality grades of plywood. "A-Grade" is the best, being well sanded with all knotholes filled with wood inserts. "Marine Grade" is actually a bit stronger (and more expensive), but its advantages are better suited for building boats, and it's not really worth the extra money for use in a house. The grades gradually deteriorate down to "D-Grade" (knotholes open to the world) and even "Shop Grade" (appearing a little like a much-used target for large-bore cannons). Usually you'll find sheets with one grade on one surface and another on the opposite side, the feeling being that in most projects only one side will show. So you can buy a sheet with "A-Grade" on one surface and "D" on the other, if need be.

A good, all-purpose grade is "Exterior, A-C Grade." There is one great danger in buying cheaper grades for a special job and that is the fact that you'll almost certainly have scraps left over with no labels on them to warn you that they're of a cheap grade. These scraps usually get used in a way that they shouldn't, and then start to come apart, surprisingly enough, and ruin your project at a later date. So it's a good idea to invest in the small added cost of keeping good plywood on hand, for you never know where you'll end up using the leftovers.

Again, you can find both special sizes and specially surfaced plywoods at a hardwood specialty lumberyard. There you can order the special "MDO Grade" plywood that is surfaced on one side with a hard, smooth overlay that is well suited for projects that must be absolutely smooth for a mirror-gloss paint finish.

When buying a stack of paneling, try to take a look at the finished surface of each sheet before they're loaded in. It doesn't happen that often, but occasionally a panel is flawed in manufacture or handling and it saves much time and disappointment to check things over before trucking the stuff home.

Almost all paneling is scored lengthwise with grooves spaced sixteen inches apart. There are additional grooves to lend a random look to the piece, but it's the grooves spaced sixteen inches in from each side that serve as guides for nailing the paneling to the wall studs, which are also spaced at sixteen-inch intervals behind the wall siding.

"Mismatched" paneling is manufactured with a different grain showing between each pair of grooves. It's a bit more expensive, but it creates a much more interesting wall. Economy paneling, with a single grain color throughout the sheets, tends to vary slightly in shade from panel to panel. Unless you're lucky, a long wall may well look like a bunch of 4 x 8 sheets tacked up. But mismatched has varied shades of grain within each sheet, making it impossible to tell where one sheet ends and the next starts.

Finding Building Bargains

In the "Building Materials" section in the classified ads of most newspapers can be found occasional announcements of fantastic bargains in all sorts of building supplies. They are usually found in little out-of-the-way lumberyards that have discovered a large batch of some sort of building material at a good price. The amount they have to buy is more than they would normally stock, so they're always anxious to move the stuff fast at a small profit per unit.

You may have to drive a few extra miles, but there are times when it's worth the gas. The materials sold are generally as good as can be found anywhere; but you have to keep your eye on the ads and act in a hurry when you find someone offering what you can use. It's priced to sell fast, and it does.

You can sometimes find supplies in these ads that you don't normally find at the local builder's supply house. Materials like unfinished paneling can be a great saving to the rebuilder. This type of paneling is actually finished smooth but hasn't been stained or varnished. By painting on a bit of stain and wiping it off each panel, you can often get elegant, mismatched panels with beautiful grain for just a little more than the cost of the prefinished economy stuff.

The bargains can range all the way from a certain shade of paint to a certain size of lumber to bathroom fixtures, depending on what bargain lots of materials happen to be on the market that week. You can usually find what you're looking for if you watch the ads long enough.

One of the greatest treasures in the eyes of the amateur builder is a good used-lumber or house-wrecking yard. In a well-stocked yard full of used wood you can browse among the delights of real hardwood, solid doors; wooden window frames in all manner of shapes and sizes; boxes filled with fascinating old solid cast doorknobs and window hardware; plate-glass mirrors that can often be cut down to size at a great saving; and lighting fixtures galore.

Used lumber is a completely different species of wood from the kind you buy new. Some of it comes from stately old houses that date back quite a way, and there's no telling what sort of interesting pieces you can find in a stack of good used lumber to build a whole new design style around. Just to wander through fascinating stacks of relics is usually enough to trip off a number of brainstorms that could add a little interest to your house.

Used lumber is extremely wellcured, naturally enough, which means it will be easy to saw, hard to nail, and won't split or shrink once it's nailed in place. One of the strangest things about the old boards (besides their lightness and strength) is that a 2" x 4" actually measures two inches by four inches—instead of 1-5/8" by 3-1/2"as they do nowadays. It must have something to do with inflation or something—who knows? Most of the lumber in used-lumber yards is recently used stuff, however, and comes in all the shriveled, popular modern sizes.

The real bargains to be searched for in a used-lumber yard are the special-size and special-texture boards that you either simply can't find or have to pay for through the nose to get from a regular lumberyard. Things like big, rough-hewn timbers, solid hardwood doors, banister posts and the like are the real discoveries.

As many people know, most larger pieces of lumber or timbers are rough-cut to size and then planed smooth in a later process somewhere down the line, either at the mill or at the lumberyard itself. But for some strange business reason you are often charged much more for a "rough-cut" piece than you are for one that's been put through the additional planing process. It's probably because of the fact that most people want the smooth timbers, and that makes rough-hewn timbers somehow special—and therefore worth more money.

If you're looking for rough-hewn timbers to create an interesting texture effect, the used-lumber yard is your savior. There, rough timbers are a pain in the neck because they have to be planed down to get the average person to buy them. So the used-lumber yards are all too glad to sell you some at a reasonable price—if they have any.

Therein lies the big drawback to the used-supply dealer—he has to take what he can get from the wrecking jobs offered him. You, in turn, have to take the bargains he offers as you find them, in most cases. There's not much hope of getting a used yard to order any materials that they don't already have sitting around.

If you're even thinking about doing some building projects, it's often a good idea just to visit the local wrecking yards and spend a little time checking over their supply from time to time. As with the bargains advertised in the papers, you can never tell how long a material will last before someone nabs it. Some interesting materials may go out the same day they come in. In other cases we've bought part of a supply of a certain material and then have gone back ten years later to buy the rest of the batch; so it's hard to tell.

When working with used lumber, you have to be careful of hidden nails or you may easily ruin a saw blade in short order. Instead of checking the boards all over as you start out, wait until you have the cut-lines marked and then check all around these lines for signs of nails that might angle across the path of the blade.

If you find yourself working with a really limited budget, or want to get the absolute maximum out of your building dollar, keep your eyes open for any sign of renovation projects in your area. If a large building is being torn down or rebuilt, then one of the local wrecking yards will usually be in charge, and you can sometimes work a good deal with the wreckers for you to pick up the material where they get it instead of where they have to take it to wait for sale.

If the renovation is a smaller job (or even a private house owner ripping out a fence), then you can often get the material free with a little amiable chitchat and some help cleaning up the area. So learn to train your eye to spot those doors that are being thrown away and that perfectly good window frame that nobody else seems to want. Saving them from the trashman can be your contribution to the recycling process.

Paints and Painting

Before moving on to choosing the right paints for your purposes, it may be a good idea to check the paint you already have sitting around. After a year or so in the garage even the best paints can become hard to work with. So be suspicious if cans are so old you can't quite remember when you bought them. Old paint can curdle and lose its life, so it's usually worth the money to start off a new project with new paint.

Modern paints have completely revolutionized the whole process of painting. Good examples of the latest developments in the world of paints cover amazingly well, resist dripping, dry rapidly, clean up easily, and most important (to some of us), they don't smell so foul as paints have over the years. Semigloss, water base paints have slightly different characteristics than

28

the flat, latex variety (we'll go into the details of this later on); but there are a few general rules for buying paints that we've found helpful.

An inexpensive screen like this one made from plastic sheeting and battens ripped on a table saw can be the quickest and easiest way to cover exposed plumbing or wiring in a playroom. With lights mounted on the wall behind, the screen can double as a light source. If you don't have a table saw, battens can be found in the molding section of lumber and supply yards.

Paints vary a good deal from brand to brand. Since a good quality paint can do more than anything else to make a job smooth, easy and highly rewarding, you could almost say that half the job is in choosing a good paint. This process would be easier if the best paint were the most expensive, and the worst the least expensive. But the fact is that *some* very inexpensive paints are among the best on the market, whereas *some* others that cost a bundle may turn out to be pretty unsatisfactory. You can't go by price alone.

What can you go by? Well, you can ask for the advice of somebody who should know, but that's pretty risky, especially if the advisor is also a seller of paints. If you don't already have a brand that you like, one of the better ways of finding a favorite is to buy just a pint or so of the various contenders in the shades that approximately match what you're looking for. Try them as a base coat, with a little bit of one brand here and a little of another there. A good paint will mix smoothly and easily and will spread on with little drag on the brush. A good paint will also resist dripping on vertical surfaces and will never show signs of separating back into the pigment and the carrier (as some poor quality paints will) once it's on the wall. A good paint will cover well and resist breaking into "fish-eye" pockmarks at the drop of a hat.

However, even a high quality paint won't really do as good a job of covering in one coat as it will with two coats. There are a number of paints "guaranteed to cover in one coat" on the market and some of them are very good, but except in the most optimistic circumstances, they won't really do the job of covering in a single coat. Even if you can spend the extra time and attention to coax a paint to look passable after only one coat, it will invariably look better and have more life and depth of color and will last longer if you add a second coat.

A paint that covers well in two coats is all we ask for, and although many perform this with no visible trouble, there are still paints on the market that, unfortunately, won't do a good job of covering with four coats.

Most latex paints (even the best) will look a little transparent and unsatisfactory just a little while after the first coat has been put on. They will start to cover most defects with the second coat. But then as they begin to dry, for some strange chemical reason they may start to display the old flaws in the wall right through the new paint again. The next day, when the paint is finally dried, the flaws are somehow hidden again. So give the second coat a chance to dry thoroughly before heading out to buy paint for a third coat.

This testing process of the different brands may seem a bit involved, but a good paint makes the work easy, and once you've found a brand that you like and have become accustomed to its characteristics, you won't have to repeat the procedure. We'll get into more specific suggestions concerning painting methods and preparations in later chapters where the techniques are used.

Tools

What tools do you need to get under way? Nothing fancy—just a basic set of hand tools will get you through. It's better to have a few good tools than a whole garage full of cheap products that will let you down. You'll end up buying the quality tool in the long run anyway, so the only way to really save money is to avoid buying the bargain tool in the first place.

One way to save money on tools is to watch the ads in the paper for tool sets offered for sale by private parties. It's usually the only way to buy real bargains. The tools you find in hock shops and secondhand stores are sometimes priced above the list price for the *brand new* tool. Many people think that because they're buying something in a dingy-looking secondhand store, the price must be a bargain; so check the costs in the catalogues before you start out for the hock shops.

Most people have enough tools lying around the house to get many of the jobs done; but for those who don't seem to have a favorite hammer to call their own, here is a suggested list of tools that we've found helpful for rebuilding houses. You don't need all of these, of course, for most jobs, so we've listed them in the approximate order of importance as all-around aids.

It's usually a good idea to buy your tools a little at a time as you need them. When you have a clear idea in mind of how you'll be using a particular tool, you'll find it easier to pick out just the pipe wrench or set of pliers that will do the job best for you.

TOOLS NEEDED FOR THE BASIC SURVIVAL OF ANY HOUSEHOLD

Carpenter's Claw Hammer
Set of good quality Screwdrivers (large and small Phillips Head and large and
   small regular variety)
10" Crescent Wrench
Medium Size Pipe Wrench
Channel-Lock Pliers

ADDITIONAL TOOLS NEEDED TO MAKE UP BASIC
HOUSE REBUILDER'S TOOL KIT

Tool box
Measuring Tape and Yardstick
Carpenter's Cross-Cut Saw
Standard Type Pliers
Long-nosed Wiring Pliers
Wood Chisel
Framing Square
3/8" Electric Drill
Electric Circular Handsaw with "Combination" Blade
Set of 1/8" to 1/2" twist drill bits
Set of 3/8" to 1-1/4" spade wood drill bits
Hacksaw (with high quality blades)
Level
Tube of DAP sealer
Hot Glue Gun

THE ART OF MAKING HOUSES LIVEABLE

ADDITIONAL TOOLS NEEDED TO FILL OUT COMPLETE
HOUSE REBUILDER'S TOOL KIT

Miter Box
Assorted special-use Screwdrivers (short and fat, long and skinny, and so on)
A second Pipe Wrench
Cabinetmaker's Square
Wire Snips (Diagonals)
Razor Knife with replaceable blades
Putty Knife
Center Punch
Linoleum Knife
Cold Chisel
Serrated Hand Shaper
Serrated Drum Shaper for Electric Drill
Keyhole Saw
Drum Hole Saw for Electric Drill
Open-End Wrench Set
Electric Saber Saw
"Yankee" Screwdriver
Electric Table Saw
Band Saw
Metal Shears
Sink Faucet Removal Wrench

The approximate order of importance depends on what job you happen to be starting with. The toolbox mentioned is truly worth the money, for it is a way of cutting your work time in half by keeping all the tools in one place where they can be found when needed. You may prefer to set up a tool board covered with your creative instruments (with outlines of the tools drawn on the board to show where the tools are hung and which ones are missing). However, if you have jobs at various ends of the house, a toolbox can be handier for getting everything to the job in one trip. Of course, if you have all the tools listed above, you may have a hard time getting them into one box, and an even harder time lifting the box once it's loaded. In this case a supplementary tool board for those special-purpose tools can take the load off the toolbox, which carries the general-purpose tools.

The main goal is to save time chasing back and forth after forgotten or missing tools. Spending a morning hunting for a wrench is the worst possible way to get rolling on a project, but it's a strangely familiar one.

Once you have a well-stocked toolbox, you may want to place a small box of assorted screws, nails, staples and washers somewhere in the bottom of the box. These odds and ends can save you much running around and even extra trips to the lumberyard when you need only one or two fasteners to get to the next step of the project.

Painting requires its own set of tools, of course, and although the tools included aren't numerous, it's important that they be of reasonably high quality in order to make the job much easier. With a good brush that doesn't spread its bristles throughout the work and allows easy border trim control, a painting job can be over before you know it. But with a cheap brush, or even a brush of the wrong size, a painting project can become a test of the soul.

Special new devices to speed up the sometimes lengthy job of painting around the edge-trim come and go on the market. Some of them work better than others, but generally, although these tools are suitable enough for such projects as painting dull, standardized apartments, they leave the look of a hurried professional. In your own house, where you have to live from day to day with the results of your work, it's usually better to stay away from these "time savers." They're not much help if you're looking for the old-world craftsman touch for your home.

BASIC PAINTING TOOLS NEEDED

2-Inch angle-cut Trim Brush
3-Inch Brush
Roller handle and sleeves (read the labels on the covers to find ones suited to your paint and wall surface
Roller Pan
Roller Handle Extension Pole
Drop Cloths (store-bought, or use old blankets or curtains)
Can of ready-mixed spackle
Putty Knife
Sheets of medium and fine Sandpaper
Masking Tape

SUPPLEMENTAL TOOLS

There are other special tools for special jobs, of course. But if you're going to be faced with a certain specialized job only once or twice, it might be better to rent the necessary tools rather than put out hard-earned cash for seldom used equipment. Power sanders, carpet laying tools, cement mixers and the like can usually be found at either lumber supply yards or equipment rental yards at a reasonable cost (and sometimes even cheaper if you can arrange a weekend rate).

There is another little-mentioned and often overlooked building aid that can save more time and money than you might imagine—namely, a well-stocked junk pile where you can throw the larger leftovers and scraps at the end of any job. If you can find an area that isn't too prominent where you can store the stuff, it will repay you handsomely. What appears to be a worthless candidate for the fireplace at the end of one project may well come in handy for getting another project under way somewhere down the line.

If you have to travel to the lumberyard for every small stick of wood and every nail and bolt, even when you need only a small amount to carry you through, project costs can skyrocket. So try to arrange a few tin cans where you can throw leftover nails, screws, hinges, and so forth, for future reference.

Any board or scrap of plywood that's bigger than a breadbox should be saved if you're serious about cutting costs. Only after you get used to the luxury of a well-stocked junk pile (that can often be a lifesaver when the stores are closed) will you appreciate how hard it is to build anything at a reasonable cost without one. If spare nails, screws and such are to be saved in containers which are open to the elements, punch holes in the bottoms of the containers so that water can drain out to prevent everything inside from rusting into one solid ball. Once you build up a backlog of fasteners and wood scraps, there will be many times when you'll be able to carry out a whole project without a single trip to your local lumberyard.

Whether you establish a junk pile or simply set up your own storage for leftover fasteners and the like, the main thing is to avoid buying the few you need for each project at the high prices that are charged for small packages of nails, screws and such.

We've found that there are generally a few standard sizes of fasteners that are the handiest for most building jobs. With a supply of 1-1/2-inch and 2-inch finishing nails; 2-inch and 3-inch galvanized box nails; and 1-1/4-inch number eight flathead wood screws, you can put together practically any kind of house project. Buying nails five pounds at a time and screws by the gross saves not only money but time.

Getting Things Rolling

Once you start to get your design ideas down in reasonably clear form and have your tools and materials in hand, the only thing that stands between you and the finished product is a little well-directed effort. What is usually needed to harness your talents to get the kind of results you're looking for is a plan of action that fits your own work habits. As with practically anything else, there are a few simple rules for this process that can make the whole project easier and more rewarding.

Most projects are a combination of tasks that fall into one of two categories: those jobs that are absolutely necessary but which might be considered time consuming, even tedious, and do very little to change the visible appearance of the surroundings; and those jobs which provide a great amount of visual change per hour of work spent.

Of course, what may seem tedious to one builder can be another's cup of tea. So the same tasks may be found in different categories, according to the tastes of the individual. But whether you enjoy a job or find it tiresome, it's a good idea to examine carefully in the light of your own preference the tasks involved in the project.

In some projects there is a set sequence of steps that can't be changed without risk of catastrophe. And in most projects there is a sequence of steps that could be considered the most logical—the sequence that prevents repeated effort and unnecessary backtracking, like putting the carpeting in *after* the wallpapering is finished. However, strangely enough, what may be

Using contrasting wall textures next to each other can sometimes bring out the best in both. Here, the spread-with-your-hands plaster texture complements the deep, rich tones of mismatched paneling, stained by the builder at a good saving of cash (as described).

the most logical and efficient sequence of steps for a seasoned pro may not be the most effective one to get the best work out of a beginning builder.

To get the best possible flow of ideas, the amateur builder may want to begin with his "knowns," despite the fact that the task involving the "known" may come far down the logical-sequence list of tasks (such as putting in a carpet color that you *know* you want to use, and *then* figuring out what color wallpaper to use with it). Financial considerations may also influence the sequence of jobs in a rebuilding project.

The most important consideration in choosing a sequence of tasks (if you have a choice) is the artist's morale. There is no substitute for enthusiasm when it comes to producing remarkable results with little experience and expense. The beginner should use every trick in the book to help himself keep up his interest in the work. It's precisely this interest and enthusiasm that will make the difference between a rich, imaginative project and an obviously inexperienced imitation of professional methods.

To help keep enthusiasm up, consider carefully which tasks of the project will probably provide the best return of visual reward for the amount of work spent. Perhaps it may help to list the tasks involved, noting the degree of

35

reward or difficulty each one seems to pose. As time goes on, this process becomes easier and is done almost unconsciously when you first size up a job.

Once you have a general idea of what is facing you in the way of fun vs. tedium, work out a simple, rough plan that will dribble the rewards out to you a little at a time, if possible, to help get you over the rough parts. If you're having trouble getting your feet wet, start out with one of the "fun" jobs—one that will provide a good visual reward. Whenever possible, however, hold the more interesting jobs back toward the end of the sequence to keep the creative interest flowing once the first flush of enthusiasm has begun to wear a little thin. The amount of concentrated motivation you can pour into a project will do more than any miracle material or supertool can to create an attractive effect. Any way you can find to keep morale up will show in the final product.

How Not To Sweat the Small Stuff

What we're shooting for throughout this whole process of rebuilding a house can be judged in terms of "Total Improvement Gained." In some jobs where the inspiration or financing is found to be lacking, a job may not be carried out in the best of all possible ways. But if it's an improvement and adds in a reasonably permanent way to the total attractiveness of the house, then you're ahead in the game. It's impossible to look for perfection in every corner of the house and expect to get the thing completed within any measurable period of time. So, if you're dealing within limits of budget, experience and materials, don't let frustration from a lack of perfection keep you from getting under way. If you keep at the limited improvements long enough, the whole effect will begin to near the goals you have in mind.

As most people know, the great innovative or inventive geniuses have tended to be a little rough around the edges in both their work and personal lives. Once their original breakthroughs received the necessary recognition, they left others to fiddle with the fine tuning. On the other hand, the great performers who have excelled in fine detail of execution generally haven't been a wellspring of new concepts. There are a few exceptions, of course— men who gained recognition for both their original ideas and their fine finish work. But history has usually shown that once a fellow gets known for one thing, he relaxes a bit on the other.

If you look at the design of appealing furniture or houses, you'll find that much the same sort of thing is true. Some old pieces with a strange, lasting attraction are found to be completely asymmetrical, with one side completely different from the other when carefully measured. Moreover, it isn't unusual to find handsome old buildings to be completely out of square and rife with what a modern inspector would call "mistakes." Still, the appeal is there despite a line that may not be absolutely straight or a ledge that isn't level. In visual things it's the basic concept, not the exact finish of detail, that makes or breaks the good effect of an object.

It doesn't make the slightest difference that one fender of a classic Bugatti is somewhat different in shape from the one on the other side of the car. The designer had the right basic concept in mind—and you can't see an object from both sides at once anyway! So the appeal of the car lasts, whereas some other, more perfectly standardized cars of the same period are better forgotten.

Once you begin to realize that the success of most visual projects doesn't depend on their degree of perfectly executed fine finish, then the whole

This shadowbox example has become almost buried under spices and cookbooks—illustrating that in a kitchen, form can sometimes be overwhelmed by function. So keep your designs simple near the areas of action.

process of building pleasant surroundings becomes more fun. We tend to worship straight lines, flat surfaces and square corners—sometimes simply because they're *there*. We can use simple tests to tell when a line isn't straight or when a surface isn't flat or a corner isn't square, but how can you tell whether a freehand curve is right or wrong?

So we often stick with those things we can judge absolutely—whether they have any basic appeal or not. However, once you take a look at those classic objects which continue to delight us over the years, you find that their pleasant effect depends on concept more than detail. Further, they even *avoid* straight lines, flat surfaces and square corners. The Greeks knew this, and even when they wanted a straight, boxy effect, they made use of certain curves and irregularities that enhanced the overall look. Once we learn that *all* optics are illusion, that there are many times when a gentle curve will look straighter than a true straight line, then we begin to lose a little respect for those mechanical straight lines.

So don't "sweat" the small stuff. Don't worry so much about getting the details perfect that you forget all about whether the basic idea is worthwhile or not. Proficiency will grow naturally with practice as you carry out your design ideas.

If the project has to function, like a sliding drawer or a cabinet door, then you can worry about getting things lined up so that they work. But if the project is just to sit there and look nice, like a shelf or a built-in table, then try to keep away from boxy straight lines and don't worry if it comes out a little lopsided so long as it looks right to you.

Work Sequences Within Each Job

Choosing the right place to begin a job can have much to do with the final result of your work. A pro knows that if the job requires a bit of warming up before you hit your stride, you should start in an inconspicuous place and work toward the area that will stand out. So if you're painting the trim around a set of cabinets (and if it's been a while since you've done that sort of thing), begin where it won't show much, and work toward the most prominent parts. This seems childishly obvious when written down, but it's a rule that most of us forget anyway.

Slow Down

One of the oldest and most important rules for doing handwork is to *slow down*. There's not a job in the whole house that can't be finished better, more enjoyably and often in less time by simply going slowly. In building it's nearly always a case of the tortoise and the hare. It takes longer to rip through a job and then clean up the resultant mistakes and mess than it does to proceed with calm, deliberation.

Go slowly and steadily; you'll be amazed at how things suddenly stop fighting you and begin to fit together with an astonishing lack of calamities. When we first took the advice and tried it, we noticed a strange feeling of anticlimax. The job was obviously finished, yet our voices weren't hoarse from yells of anguish, we weren't sweating from unconcealed rage—we weren't even breathing hard. Somehow the job was done and we still had time for a little concentrated loafing. "Slow Down" sounds like such a simple rule; nevertheless, it's a hard lesson to keep in mind in the heat of action.

Pondering

It sometimes happens that you find yourself standing starry-eyed, looking off into the middle distance just before ripping into a new project. We've found that this staring period can sometimes be more profitable than it might appear to the casual bystander. This contemplative lull before the action can sometimes lead to further solutions that will speed the completion of the project in its later stages. If there seem to be so many unanswered questions that beginning a project is out of the question, then schedule some meditation time in which you can stare at the problem area for a goodish amount of time. If anyone asks you what you think you're doing, you can tell them you're hard at work and show them this part of the book to prove it.

What To Do in Case of That Rare Occurrence: The Goof

Goofs have a way of sneaking into the most experienced builder's work. Even if you try diligently to ban them from your design and execution, a few will occasionally slip by. So it's really a question of what to do *when* you goof, not *if* you goof. Napoleon (or one of those military masterminds) once said that a great general is not one who never makes mistakes (which is uncommon) but rather one who quickly recognizes his mistakes and acts to correct them.

The first thing to do, however, is to make sure you really *have* goofed. If you begin to believe that you've made a mistake in the whole design concept, it's sometimes better to put off final judgment until the job is complete enough to give the new look a chance. This doesn't mean painting the whole house with a color you've suddenly begun to hate; but do a large enough area to get a real idea of the finished effect before scratching the project. When you can no longer see the old shade of paint (at least in one area), the new hue may begin to look a little more like what you had in mind in the first place.

Of course, the best way to cope with mistakes is to use methods that help show them up before you commit yourself. As we've said before, cardboard or paneling mock-ups of proposed room dividers, closets, built-in furniture, and the like, can make decisions much more obvious than they would appear on paper. You can approximate paint shades with colored sheets of construction paper, hanging a sheet or two on the walls in question to get an idea of the effect. Even blankets of a shade similar to the one that you're thinking about will work. If you can borrow the whole wallpaper sample book you can prop it up, opened to the paper you think you like, and leave it there for a day or so to see how it will work out.

Knowing how to get the most out of mock-ups and sample tests is also important. The shock test is one of the best ways to make your preferences

39

clear and the decisions easier to make. In doing a shock test, fix a mock-up or sample panel in place and then walk away and forget about it. Work on something else, watch TV, or do anything (within reason) to forget the design question at hand. In due course of your wanderings you will suddenly happen on the propped up sample, and it will cause some sort of obvious reaction in you. It's this unprepared, unbiased reaction that you're hunting for, so try your best, as soon as the shock is over, to remember and define the reaction that the mock-up brought out in you. You may want to change a few details and then repeat the shock process until you get the reaction you want.

Another test is the mirror test. To make use of this, simply hold up a hand mirror so you can see the area in question reflected in it. Somehow, viewing things backward, especially rooms you are well accustomed to, will give you an entirely new outlook—and often the solution to how to finish the room. If you have a camera with a viewfinder that reverses the field, this can also be used to get a new vantage point and possibly a new answer.

If it seems hard to define just where a divider wall or bar or built-in should be located, try placing the mock-up reasonably close to where you think it should go, and then start moving it until you know it's too far to one side; mark this spot. Next move it in the opposite direction until you know it is too far to the other side, then mark this position. By moving the mock-up back and forth between these limits, you can narrow the limits until you know within a few inches where you want it to go.

The same is true with any project involving placement proportions. Try making the mock-up of the bar longer and longer until it's obviously too long. Then shorten it until it's obviously too short. Finally, narrow your limits until you know how it should be. Often you'll find the final positioning to be at the midway point between the first two limits you set.

It's undeniably hard sometimes to admit that one of your brainstorms is a loser, especially after investing a bit of cash and hard labor in the process. (We once lived with a wallpaper sample book for a week studying a pattern; tried all the tests; were sure we liked it; went ahead and ordered the paper; put it up—and hated it instantly!)

However, honesty is the best policy when it comes to dealing with these design duds. When an idea just doesn't seem to work out in practice, you'll find your mind performing all sorts of tricks and double-jointed rationalizations in an effort to persuade yourself to like an obvious mistake. If you can be honest with yourself and flexible enough to admit that maybe your project didn't quite work out in practice, you'll be well on your way to making those changes and minor adjustments that can oftentimes save it.

If a wallpaper or a paint color is a bit overwhelming, perhaps reducing the area covered by the color or paper can soften the blow yet keep the original concept intact. Sometimes changing accessories in the room will solve the problem, such as a different shade of curtains or bedspreads. Unfortunately, there are very rare occasions when nothing will help, and then you just have to wait until you have the necessary time and money to start all over again. Generally speaking, there are usually a number of modifications open to you which can save the original concept, but to make use of these, you have to have a clear idea of exactly where the trouble lies. This involves the sometimes

Inexpensive built-in work benches can be made from stained fir, with cupboard door fronts cut from a type of plywood called "Texture 1-11."

painful process of being scrupulously honest with yourself. It's good for the soul, though, they tell us.

Teamwork

If you're planning to work in concert with others as a team, there are several rules for making the whole process workable that will become evident after a while.

We've found that it's usually a good idea to split up and specialize rather than try to share equally in every enlightening experience. This will keep everyone out of everyone else's hair and will give the team members a choice of jobs. It will also permit you to get more work accomplished than you could have done by yourself, which is not the case with most committee-building.

People vary greatly in work interests and talents; by splitting up to work on separate tasks, you'll get the right man for the right job. Advice will be given only when asked for, and everyone will tend to be a great deal more cordial at the end of the day.

When you fall into the obvious trap of having everybody try to work together on every step, you tend to spend most of your time arguing. Even after the wheels do begin to turn, you slowly develop an inability to work without an audience. Some of us have been known to make a bigger noise about everyday mistakes when there is someone handy to hang on every word.

If you're working consistently as a team, you may begin to notice that one member seems to find a certain type of job easy, while the others may excel in different directions. When this happens, the work of the expert in each area should be followed unless there are strenuous objections from the loyal opposition. For example, we learned that one of us can handle designing shape and form, whereas the other is much better at questions of color and texture. In most cases we bow to the other's judgment within his or her own particular forte. But if either is suddenly possessed by a brainstorm that reaches into the other's field, he can go ahead and override all objections. However, if the person struck by the brainstorm isn't absolutely positive, it's better for him to just make suggestions and then let the expert in the area have the final say. We've found these rules help keep debating to a minimum yet allow enough flexibility for the occasional stroke of genius to come through without fear of compromise. For compromise is what tends to take all strength, authority and fun out of creating your own surroundings. It's better for everybody to have his own little corner just the way he wants it than for everyone to join in on every single decision.

Critical Phases

Most projects go through two critical periods in their process of becoming tangible additions to the house. The first occurs at the start when you begin to limber up your mind for the challenge of working with your hands.

If you haven't done any handwork for some time, there is always a period of adjustment for changing your work habits from mental to physical. And this seems to take place, no matter how impressive your last bit of work happened to be.

The fact is, working with our hands seems to teach us one set of rules, whereas working mentally or verbally, as most of us do in our jobs, often teaches us another. But whatever talents we learn from the rest of life, working with our hands will teach us to be honest in our work, if nothing else. You can't argue with a measuring tape—either the thing fits or it doesn't.

So the first few hours of many projects are often spent coming to the realization that you can't bluff your way through when you're building something. The process will take less time, of course, if you've already gone through it on a number of occasions; nevertheless, much of the first day of work may be spent just "getting under way" or readjusting yourself to the simple, honest world of building. For that reason you generally can't expect to get too much accomplished on your first day out. On the second day of work you will probably get more than twice as much accomplished as on the first. So it's usually a good idea to arrange your schedule to have at least two consecutive days of work. If possible, it's better to work one whole weekend on a project and then take the following weekend entirely off than to work one day of each weekend.

The second crisis comes just as you're bringing the project to a conclusion, and the time approaches when the results of your measuring and planning either will fit magically together or won't—the moment which in other endeavors is called "The Moment of Truth."

Unfortunately, in most projects the truth is that the parts almost never fall magically into place—no matter how careful you have been. Oh, it happens once in a while, it's true; but it's a rare event, and good cause for celebration.

Usually there are a number of tiny quasi-mistakes that no one can really be blamed for, which must be adjusted before the piece will, in fact, fit together and work. This is no sign of a lack of attention or talent on the part of the builder; it's simply a combination of those little factors that you really can't plan on, or allow for, while building. In the great majority of projects we've seen (no matter how skilled the builder may be), there is at the end almost always a short, feverish period of minor adjustments and pushing and pulling until the thing finally falls into place.

As one seasoned building expert put it, "You do every step exactly right, and then you kick it until it works." The only real drawback to this train of events is that newcomers to building aren't prepared for this added step. They follow all the prescribed instructions, but for some exasperating reason the thing won't fit together. Then they often quit the field in disgust, whereas a pro simply realizes that it's time for him to leave the rules and make use of his native intuition and common sense to bring about those final small changes that will make the project a success. So if everything doesn't quite come together after you've completed each step carefully, don't reach for the revolver. It's just time to start kicking it to show who's boss.

Barn Raising

In the days of yore it was the custom among farm folk, as everybody knows, to band together once in a while to help one of the community get a certain large job done in a hurry—and to create a bit of festive atmosphere in the process. This same Barn Raising method works just as well today as it ever did, and it's still just as much fun.

The secret of the Barn Raising's success is that it's somehow much easier to cope with the problems of somebody else's house than it is to tackle those lengthy projects looming up in your own. A job that requires many hours of simple but tedious labor may be filling your heart with dread. A well-organized Barn Raising can solve the whole problem in a single day, and it can be cause for a lot of fun in the bargain.

We've seen entire houses painted, interiors cleaned and refurbished, and even whole room additions put up in a single day of Barn Raising. And the strange part is, everyone invariably ends up telling the host that it's the best party he's given for years.

Of course, it isn't as simple as calling everybody up and then standing back to watch the progress. There are a few hints to making a Barn Raising work, and the formula that we've seen work goes something like this:

The most important thing is that the work should progress with as few interruptions as possible. Once the thread of action is broken, it's hard to get everyone rolling again. So make certain that all design decisions and time-consuming preparations are made in advance so that when the Barn Raising day dawns, there is nothing to stop the progress.

There should be ample food and refreshments prominently displayed to bolster morale through times of crisis (withholding any alcoholic rewards until the tools have been put away). The main function of the owner of the house is really one of making sure that everyone is well supplied with the necessary materials and equipment—and refreshments—at all times.

Many hands make light work, and you can pack an amazing amount of accomplishment into one day of Barn Raising with four to six, or maybe eight, helpers. But don't try to expand it into a C. B. DeMille production. If you get more helpers than you need for the job, you'll end up with half the crew standing around with nothing to do but distract the other half. A reasonably small crew of four to six seems to work out best.

One day of Barn Raising is a lark, but two days are work; so with a couple of careful guesses you have to gauge approximately how much you can hope to get done in a single day and how many workers will make up a good crew. We've found that you can generally be optimistic about the amount of work you can expect from a day of Barn Raising. For example, the exterior of an average house can be painted in a day, provided the surfaces are prepared and the eaves are done ahead of time.

Not every job lends itself to a Barn Raising, of course. Tasks requiring great concentration or a certain amount of prior practice are usually ruled out. But those big, time-consuming and basically simple jobs, like painting, laying cement, roofing, laying patio flooring, moving furniture, and the like, can usually be handled nicely by a Barn Raising crew. Because they won't take the job as seriously as you would tend to, they will work like troopers to show you how simple the whole thing is, and how silly you were to dread the project in the first place.

Barn Raisings are reciprocal, of course, and once others begin to see the advantages of the whole process, you'll most likely find yourself a carefree, well-fed member of someone else's Barn Raising crew before too long. It's a good excuse for the womenfolk to get together and drum up some fancy foods, and for the men to get some exercise and to demonstrate how easily they can accomplish things. There are times when a Barn Raising candidate may be a little too bashful, or a little too uncertain of his potential helpers' abilities, to organize a much needed Barn Raising for himself. In this case a few words among friends, and especially wives, can get the wheels of progress rolling. And we've never seen a Barn Raising victim (however he might doubt the sanity of the idea at first) who wasn't entirely pleased with the quality of work done.

2

Living Room Ideas

The living room is all things to all men—and an emptier term is hard to find. In a bathroom we bathe; in a bedroom we go to bed; and in a living room, we are led to believe, we live, whatever that may mean.

The criteria for a good living room are just as vague and changeable from one person's point of view as the next. One person may tell you that a living room is a place where you throw big parties, show home movies or play cards; another will tell you that it's a place where you build a canoe, clean your shotguns or rebuild those carburetors that have been giving your car fits. It all depends on what you call "living."

Most people will agree that one of the main functions of a living room is to serve as a place where you receive guests. One of the most important factors in creating a pleasant place to greet visitors is an interesting seating arrangement that lends itself to the kind of social atmosphere you're after— whether it's to be cozy and cheerful or stately and imposing.

In deciding on a basic arrangement for the room to suit your goals, you're apt to run up against a bit of interplay between your furniture and the floor plan of the room. Since the layout of a new floor plan may well outlast your existing furniture, don't worry if you don't happen to have the perfect couch for the new look just yet. All will come in time, and you can get into a lot of design trouble by changing too many of the variables at once. Instead of thinking about furniture styles at this point, it may be more worthwhile to concentrate on the general categories of furniture pieces you will want to include to create the areas and mood you want.

At this stage the task at hand is to explore all the possibilities. To bring these possibilities to mind, make use of any and all the available idea-testing aids, such as mirror viewing and mock-ups.

Once you have a general idea of how you would like to break up the volume of the room—either with built-ins and dividers or simply with furniture pieces—you can start settling the questions of color and texture effects to help create moods in the different areas of the room. Decide which areas should be bright and cheery, which should be dark, warm and cozy, and so forth.

Since most mass-built houses have adjoining living and dining-room areas, you may find that this is a good time to plan a more definite division of these spaces with a bar or shelves or a simple divider so that you don't have to limit yourself to effects that must work equally well for both places.

Dining areas are a bit tricky because they're used in widely varying light conditions, whereas a living room is used primarily in leisure hours in the great majority of cases. Some very warm and inviting living rooms can look pretty dark and cavelike against the glare of the morning sunlight. But this usually doesn't matter much if the room is seldom used except with artificial lighting.

However, a dining area needs to be as cheerful in the morning light as it is warm and inviting in the evening with the lamps on. If you have a choice when laying out the living-dining area, try to coordinate the room's use with the direction of the sunlight at the various times of day. Place the breakfast nook where it can face the morning sun, the easy chairs where you can enjoy the view of evening coming on, and so forth. Whatever you decide on, it's a mistake to ignore the moods created by the outside lighting.

Next consider the cold facts of the function of the living room in your own particular case. If you find yourself a bit overcrowded with too many books, hi-fi's, TV's and bric-a-brac in what may seem to be a laughably small area, explore the idea of space-saving wall components, built-ins and room divider shelf units.

Such projects can solve a great number of storage-display problems in an amazingly small amount of floor space, while creating a warm wall covering effect. The temptation when planning a wall component is to go to the extra trouble and expense of mounting the shelves on changeable brackets in a laudable attempt at flexibility. However, experience has shown most builders that once the shelves are in, they are never moved again. Since it's a good deal harder to make a wall component with the flexibility feature, it may be better to spend a little time testing the positioning of the shelves by propping or tacking them in place. Then go ahead and install them permanently in the combination that you like best. Check chapter 14 for one way to put in built-in wall component units, although you may come up with a variation that better suits your needs. Built-in couches providing storage space beneath the cushions can also expand the storage capacity of a small house.

While we're considering possibilities, we shouldn't forget countertop bars, both as room dividers and for use in wall components. A bar with storage below, and even cabinets hung above it, can provide not only a natural division of living and dining areas but can also supply an additional place to eat and entertain. Creating a pass-through bar window from the living-dining area into the kitchen is another possibility that could add greatly to the flexibility of the area.

The right carpeting can really make a living room, yet running the carpet up to the entryway can result in a lot of wear and tear on the rug in this area. A possibility to consider is a divider wall to one side of the door, separating a small area of floor from the main part of the living room. This entry space provides a natural division of the floor so that ceramic or linoleum tiles, or wood, can be used as a rugged flooring that will stand up better to the dirt and

Wall components—the saviors of the overcrowded room. When all seems lost and it looks as if you need three rooms to take care of what you have in one, the wall component can come to the rescue, providing a place for everything and everything in its place—including space for TV, hi-fi, books, records, record player and bric-a-brac.

mud from the outside world. The divider wall often creates a handy conversation nook on the living-room side and prevents the entry area from taking up too much of the living room proper.

Entryway closets can also be worked into such an arrangement to isolate a small tiled or wood floor area. Living-room closets, it must be admitted, take up a good deal of floor area but are a definite necessity. In most cases their somewhat bleak appearance can be made more interesting by replacing the typical paneled door with shutters, by wallpapering the door or possibly making a built-up "antique" door as shown in chapter 18.

Turning Your Ideas into Reality

When you reach the point where you have developed fairly definite ideas on how you'd like the volume of the room to be allotted and split up, you can start considering the more specific possibilities that will enable you to get the effect you have in mind.

We'll progress through all the ramifications of the various alternatives at the start of each section dealing with ways to cover walls, flooring choices, dividers, components, curtains, and so forth. If you know approximately which choices you want to make in each area, you can run a quick check to make sure one of the other alternatives wouldn't be more satisfactory. Then you can skip ahead to the construction section for the step-by-step methods of carrying out your chosen technique without having to wade through any information you may not need.

If you don't have rough ideas of what you want, then reading over the alternatives presented at each point, which also describe the work and investment involved, may well make the right choices easier.

Wall Treatments

Although there is an infinite number of ways to re-cover a wall, for the purposes of this book we'll stick to those that are within the reach of most amateur builders dealing with a typical house. Even then, your selections are many. The techniques covered in this section will include: painting, paneling, textured plaster, textured composition board, wallpaper, wall component shelves and weathered lumber paneling. There are other eye-catching coverings better suited to smaller wall areas (imitation brick, rock, fabric and shingles) and these can be found in the wall-covering part of the construction section.

Although the more eye-catching wall coverings are a bit overwhelming when used for a large section, they can work out well if you happen to have a small area of wall that seems suited to a special-interest texture. So it might be worthwhile to look over these techniques before settling on your plan of action.

Each of the following methods has its own advantages and drawbacks, of course. And like anything else, you tend to get in effect what you pay for in effort.

Painting is one of the easier ways to cover a wall, and although clean, new paint and an appealing color change can do a lot to improve a room, the change isn't quite as startling in most cases as with some of the more ambitious wall-covering methods.

Paneling is an effective way to bring about a real change in a room as well as to cover up all manner of holes and dents in the existing walls. But even the cheapest paneling is more expensive than painting, of course. Since the effect of wood paneling is fairly strong, covering all the walls of a room with paneling is not only costly; it sometimes diminishes the appeal of the wood grain interest.

A combination of the two treatments—covering some of the walls with paint and the others with paneling—makes effective complementary use of both techniques, getting the most from the wood effect while keeping costs down.

A rough textured plaster covering can also create an interesting contrasting effect in combination with paneling. In this case the technique is inexpensive, but there is a bit of effort to be reckoned with.

There are a number of new textures of masonite paneling that can create interesting effects. An example is a stucco texture panel that is used between

If you can help it, never let a wall go blank without something to relieve the monotony. Here a piece of 2' x 8' x 1/2" plywood was simply covered with a complementary shade of burlap and then framed with stained lengths of 1" x 6" to provide added shelving, a shadowbox and a bulletin board surface all in one easy project.

rough 1" x 6" or 1" x 8" "halftimbers" to get a Tudor look with a minimum of work. The drawback here is a fairly substantial cost, generally in the same range as a medium-priced to expensive paneling.

The imitation brick and rock textures vary all the way from the effective to the ridiculous. There are products on the market which create a wall effect of brick or rock that is difficult to tell from the real thing, yet they are infinitely easier to install on an existing wall. This opens up all sorts of opportunities to the amateur builder. Some come in single sheets, others come joined and are grouted around each piece to look exactly like masonry; still others are glued in place with a ready-made grout, allowing complete flexibility in the patterns of the varied shades of the pieces.

In the ridiculous category are the paper-thin vacuum-formed plastic bricks and rocks which are made up in sheets. They tend to have a phony, glossy look and collapse with one push of the finger.

So some imitations are good only for a laugh; others are worth checking into. If you don't like the idea of fakes, remember that most dry wall and plaster hollow wall combinations found in houses today are simply a stage front imitation of a solid masonry wall. If we're surrounded with fakes anyway, they might as well be attractive fakes.

Wallpaper has completely changed in the last few decades until it has reached the point where most of the old legends of catastrophes lying in wait for the unwary do-it-yourselfer are completely groundless. With all the improvements in the new pretrimmed, preglued, scrubbable varieties of wallpaper, this technique for covering a wall is one of the easiest you can choose. Again, the price for most brands is fairly steep compared with paint; but if you use it only on certain walls that seem to need added interest, you can not only heighten the effect of the paper but also keep the cost of the whole project within a limited budget.

A wall component is one of the most expensive *and* time-consuming ways to cover a wall. Yet when you consider the amount of storage and display problems that a single wall covered with component shelves can solve (not to mention the added warmth and versatility of the place), it is often well worth the cost and effort.

Weathered lumber as a wall covering creates an interesting effect, yet it is one that's best used in limited applications because of its striking appearance. You can usually find inexpensive weathered lumber, but you have to hit it lucky to come up with a large and fairly homogeneous batch. To find enough for wall-covering use, it's almost necessary to happen along when someone is tearing down an old barn.

Comparing Flooring for Living Rooms

Carpeting is the most popular choice for a living-room floor covering, and we tend to agree that it's the most versatile and appealing alternative for the room's varied uses. However, in certain design themes and in special areas of the living-dining room you may think about using a contrasting floor covering

51

to complement the carpeting and possibly lengthen its life. In entryways, high-use pathways and eating areas, a hard-gloss flooring will obviously stand up better.

Carpeting can be less of an awe-inspiring investment if you do the installation yourself, but a lot depends on your own particular situation. If you find a bargain in carpeting with no readily available means of getting it installed, you may want to do the job yourself. Or if you happen to have a room with a simple shape and a large floor area, it may also be worthwhile to do your own installation. But if you have a room with a complex shape, including stairways and other complications, then it may be a better idea to pay the dollar or so extra per yard in order to have it professionally installed. Tack-down strips and special tools are often available at lumber and supply yards, equipment rental places or carpeting and upholstery shops for a reasonable rental fee if you decide to go ahead on your own. You have to keep your wits about you, but there's no real mystery to the job if you take your time and think through each step before slicing up the carpet.

Linoleum and cork tiles for special use areas are extremely simple and relatively inexpensive to install. Ceramic Spanish tiles are not much more difficult to put down, even if there is an extra step or two in the procedure. There are new polyester imitation-stone tiles that seem to be easy to install, but they haven't been on the market long enough to demonstrate their durability in actual practice. Generally, when looking over the samples of floor-covering alternatives, you can count on most of the square linoleum tiles as being easy to put in.

Square tiles of felt and shag carpeting, despite their easy installation, have not shown that they can stand up well under heavy wear. They often end up presenting a pretty shabby appearance when the corners peel up and the borders wear away.

Any type of sheet linoleum can present a real test of the soul of an amateur builder, and few first tries look presentable. In fact, we don't think sheet linoleum gives much of an appealing effect even when perfectly laid, but this is in the area of personal preference again. Like any sheet covering, linoleum is difficult to fix when any area is burned, worn or chipped away, because the entire sheet has to be removed just to fix one damaged area.

Built-In Furniture Possibilities

A typical living room in the usual mass-built house is often a pretty stark affair and lends itself well to all sorts of built-in furniture, shelving and room divider ideas, not to mention closets, bars, planters, and even built-in dining tables, as shown in the illustrations.

Simple divider walls are a cinch to frame up out of 2" x 4"s; then they can be covered with your choice of paneling, plywood covered with wallpaper, textured plaster over dry wall, or even the usual paint over dry wall combination. The cost is low, considering the great changes it can bring about in a room.

Divider walls made up of shelf components (actually free-standing, two-sided wall components) can run into a little more money and effort, but the return is far greater in added appeal and storage and display area. Divider

If you balk at the prices for lathe-turned wood posts (as any right-thinking consumer might), square-cut posts can create just as interesting effects at a small fraction of the cost (with a little industry).

53

shelves either can be of the see-through variety or can be built with backing on one side of the shelves. You can make an interesting divider wall by planning the arrangement of the shelves to vary the side on which the backing is placed on the different shelves. In this sort of divider, the backing of a shelf on one side is a flat display surface; on the other it is for posters, paintings, photos and the like.

Divider walls can also be built up in a simple fashion from turned posts; however, these posts can run into a good deal of money if you buy them ready-made. If you're proficient with a band saw or a lathe, you may want to make your own squared or turned posts at a great saving of cash.

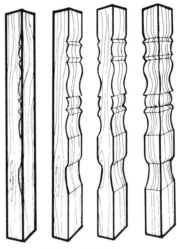

Divider Wall Posts

Wall component shelves, as we have said, are a great boon to the over-crowded living room. Made up from 1" x 10"s or 1" x 12"s (with a nice quality finish and grain), they are a fairly easy project to construct, especially considering the contribution they can make. But again, whenever dealing with large amounts of good quality lumber, the price is substantial, with costs running anywhere from $30 to $75 for an eight-to-twelve-foot unit, depending on the type of wood used. Besides providing places to store books, record players, TV's, magazines and other treasures, a wall component can include cupboard space for those needed accessories that aren't particularly intriguing to look at, such as camera equipment, photo albums and tools.

Bars with overhanging cabinets may solve a cramped living room-dining room setup by creating a divider that also provides additional eating and entertaining space. However, such a project is fairly challenging, and unless you've had experience in cabinetry, it may be better to save this project until later. Bars can also be built into wall components (even if they're not the walk-around-the-back species) with a little more ease.

Built-in couches with storage units below are simple affairs to deal with, being little more than a box with provisions for padding on top. With the interesting new textured panelings on the market, they can be the answer to

54

adding interest and storage space to an awkward corner that seems a little stark. With either hinged upholstered tops, or cupboard doors in the front, they can provide a surprising amount of storage volume for little-used memorabilia and sporting equipment.

Built-in dining tables are an inexpensive way to replace a worn out set of tables and chairs with a bold break from the traditional. Despite their relatively low cost, there is a certain amount of effort and engineering skill involved in bringing one off that is both solid and attractive.

Women are forever claiming that there's no such thing as too much closet space, and a close look at the situation often shows that the old place could stand a few more square feet of storage area. If a closet can be built onto a living room so that it helps create a new and interesting layout of the room's floor plan, then the project can be doubly worthwhile.

Built-in projects can be the perfect answer to save a dark, awkward corner while adding individuality to a room. This one was fashioned of scrap panels and 1" stock.

The process of building closets isn't much more involved than putting up a single divider wall. A 2" x 4" framing can be put up and simply covered with your favorite wall covering, and the door, or doors, attached. Once a shelf or two and a clothes rod are installed, there isn't much more to it. The step-by-step instructions for making the type of closet seen in the illustrations follow in the construction section.

If a drab window treatment, plus a cramped feeling, seems to be a problem in one area, perhaps a built-out window box can solve both with a single stroke. It's a perfect way to use old windows found at a wrecking yard, and the result can completely transform a room. Such a project, however, is the involved type that's best to tackle after you've warmed up on a few simpler tasks.

Any single-shelf or planter-box ideas are usually simple, one-day projects with no real taxing of the creative resources. But since this type of project is not the sort that brings about great changes in the basic concept of a room, it's sometimes better to put off the little things until after the fundamental plan is under way, so that they won't have to be ripped out later when found to be in the way of a bigger project.

Window treatments can often be changed with a little imaginative modification of what's already there. It's not too hard to put together interesting window inserts to provide a more appealing window frame which will fit the existing hole in the wall. New curtain treatments with easy-to-make cornice boards that tie the windows into the design of the room (either with material matching the fabric of the furniture or with matching wood finishes) can be an extremely simple way to solve the familiar problem of the stark, jail-cell window found in many houses.

Mirrors are often overlooked as a way to expand the apparent volume of a cramped room to a remarkable extent. They're in a class by themselves in their ability to add depth to a room, but of course, the high cost per square foot of a good plate glass mirror sometimes makes the price prohibitive. Installation is reasonably easy; just follow the rules in the construction section.

Large mirrors with only minor flaws around the edges can often be found at a used-supply yard, and the methods for cutting an old mirror down to get rid of its flaws are also supplied in the construction section. Large pieces of thick glass are actually much easier to cut than thinner pieces; so, if the price for the whole mirror is right, don't shy away from cutting a mirror down to size just because it's large.

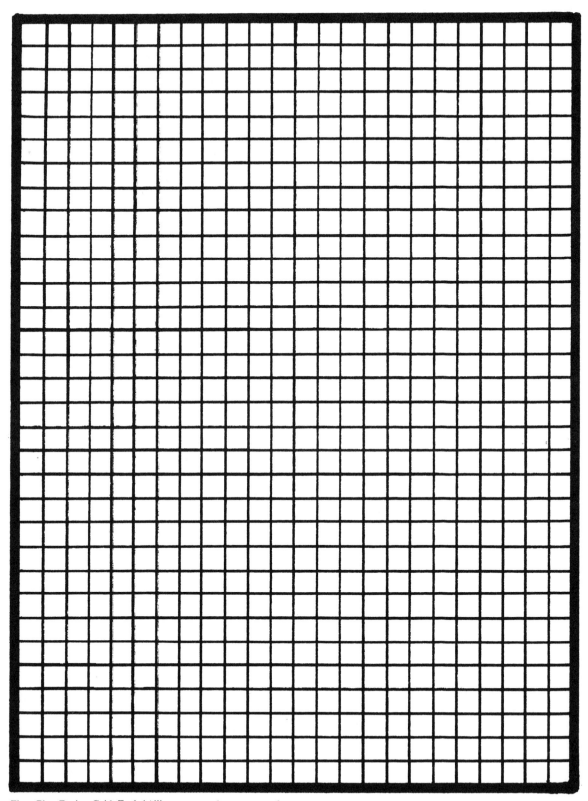

Floor Plan Design Grid. Each 1/4" square equals one square foot.

3

General Kitchen Ideas

There are those who will argue that the kitchen is the most important room in the house. Whether this is true or not will vary with your point of view (and sometimes with the time of day, of course; its importance grows measurably around mealtime). The fact remains that in many cases, much of the household activity seems to center around the kitchen; therefore it merits a good deal of your most studied thought.

As any hostess knows, the better part of the action of a good party often seems to happen in the kitchen, so there are reasons to pour a little extra effort into this room.

At first glance, a kitchen seems to be fairly inflexible, with little opportunity for creative fooling around. The larger appliance locations are usually pretty well fixed by their power outlets, vents and such. The plumbing is usually held in place by the surrounding cabinetry, and it's difficult to move a sink without rebuilding the drawers and cupboards around it. The refrigerator is generally nestled in the only remaining space, with the location of the surrounding cabinetry usually dictated by window placement and the sink and countertop positions. In short, it seems that there is little change you can make in any of the components of a kitchen without changing everything.

Total change is possible, of course, and in some extreme cases you may want to do this. But we've found that despite the sometimes helpless feeling the kitchen can give a rebuilder, much can be done to change the mood of the room by leaving the basic components in place and making the best of the design opportunities that surround them. Surprisingly, there are still many choices to play with in a kitchen, even if you leave the heavy equipment just as it is.

Because the room is usually chopped up into many small spaces and wall areas, there are often many spots just bristling with design opportunities that the original builder didn't have time to include. Because the wall areas are generally small, you can bring into play all sorts of extra-interest wall coverings that aren't suited to the large areas found in most other rooms (and which may be too expensive to use in larger doses).

So, for all their functional requirements, kitchens can still provide some of the most interesting rebuilding opportunities in the whole house.

Setting a Goal for the Rebuilding Process

Before jumping into the first project, it may be worthwhile to step back and review the role that the kitchen plays in your life. If you, or anyone in the family, like to throw yourself into your cooking, you may want to start a plan to enlarge and elaborate the cooking facilities—possibly even allowing some cooking areas to dribble out into the adjoining rooms.

If the reverse is true, and cooking is only a necessary evil, then you may want to create a concentrated, efficient little galley with nothing included that isn't absolutely needed. In this case you may be able to bring outside functions into the kitchen so that the space can be used for different interests between the short periods when the cooking is actually going on.

Before beginning, it's also a good idea to check over the fixtures to see which ones might need replacing in the near future. Naturally, it's a lot easier to replace a stove or a sink at the start of the kitchen project rather than later on when the counters or new flooring may already be in. And even if you can't see your way to replacing a worn fixture at this stage of the game, it's still a good idea to note which ones will probably have to go in the foreseeable future so that a certain degree of flexibility can be built into the projects in the surrounding areas.

If you find yourself looking through the new stoves or refrigerators on the market, don't forget to check for sources of freight-damaged fixtures. Often a perfectly good new stove can be found at a great saving just because it received a dent or two in the side en route to the store. Most of the time these dents or creases will be hidden by the surrounding cabinetry anyway.

When shopping for sinks, remember that some lumber and supply yards, or even used-supply yards, will carry brand-new factory seconds at greatly reduced prices. The flaws in these units usually amount to just a pinhole or two in the porcelain or a chip around the edge—the sort the sink will probably pick up in the first month of use anyway. Just make sure before buying that the flaw or irregularity doesn't occur around the drain flange or any water-tight plumbing hookup.

You can also run across bargains in new solid brass faucets at used lumber and supply yards, but these are mostly off-brands that may be difficult to find parts for in years to come. Whenever buying any faucet unit, go the extra money for a repair kit if it is available. You probably won't need it for years to come, but when you do, the faucet will probably be out of print and repair kits out of the question. So just hang the extra kit on a nail under the sink until it's needed.

Once you have formed definite ideas about what can or should be done with the existing stove, sink, refrigerator, disposal and dishwasher, you can start to plan the mood or setting of the kitchen.

60

Wall Treatments

Even though the small areas in a kitchen lend themselves to interesting wall coverings, we are limited somewhat in the range of choices by the conditions found in this room in the heat of the action. What is generally needed is a fire-resistant, scrubbable surface that can be cleaned easily after being exposed to the steam and grease of a kitchen.

This may rule out the use of rough natural wood texture, or fabrics—or any surface with a porous finish, for that matter. However, if your heart is set on a rough-hewn wood texture for a wall, there are some very nice textured masonite panels that will create the effect, yet can be washed clean. In fact, even if you're looking for a smooth wood paneling, you may want to think about using a masonite imitation instead of the real thing because it seems to stand up to steamy conditions better than finished wood, and the effect is almost impossible to tell from that of wood paneling.

If paint is to be used, the semigloss variety is best. A flat finish paint is impossible to scrub clean, and a high gloss paint is difficult to work with because the brush strokes tend to stand out if not applied very carefully.

Wallpaper is a good wall covering for kitchens, and as we said previously, it's easier than ever to handle—especially easy in most kitchens because of the small wall areas to be covered. Vinyl-coated washable paper is the type best suited for kitchen purposes, and because it's a bit thicker than other types of paper, it's a little easier to work with.

Surfaces such as textured plaster or shingles and the like are not well suited to life in the kitchen. If a rough look is sought after, some of the imitation brick and stone products on the market are both appealing and long-lasting. The type of brick or rock that uses a real grout to fill in around the individual pieces is the most convincing. Plastic bricks which are glued on separately have also proved themselves to be durable and easy to clean.

Kitchen Flooring

What to do about a kitchen floor is much less of a problem nowadays, thanks to new products on the market, as well as new applications for old, familiar standbys normally used in other rooms. There was a time when linoleum tiles or sheet linoleum was your only choice in most typical kitchens. But the world has wised up a bit in dealing with the floors in this room and now practically anything from carpeting to flagstone can be found there.

Carpeting can add much appeal, but of course not every type can cope with the wear and tear of kitchen use (obviously, a deep-pile shag isn't the best thing to drop spaghetti on). The felt indoor-outdoor carpeting can appear very attractive when first installed; however, it tends to "pill" under heavy wear, and whenever a spill occurs, the moisture is absorbed and then hardens under the spots. Carpet "tiles" have not proved any degree of durability in actual use, and they will often curl at the edges and look rather unappealing, as well as become a hazard to navigation.

Added shelving can be a worthwhile excuse to bring heavy, textured timbers into the kitchen. Shelving can be set into horizontal notches cut in the timbers or simply nailed down to cleats as in this example.

General Kitchen Ideas

The best type of carpeting for a kitchen in our experience is a thick but short-pile commercial carpet—the type used in stores and theaters. It's rather expensive per yard, but considering the small amount of floor area in most kitchens, it may well be worth the extra investment. The traffic pattern in most kitchens is such that a tough carpet would be needed even if there were never any spills to be mopped up (and this particular rug is especially good about wiping clean).

Imitation masonry can be used to hide old tile splashboards. Time and money were saved by covering the tile with "brickwork" when new tile was installed on the horizontal counter area.

To some, this type of short, tough carpeting doesn't look quite so luxurious as a deep shag; but after years of use the shag will usually be showing its age, whereas the commercial carpet will still look much as it did when first installed.

Prewaxed cork tile is one of the easiest floorings to lay and creates a reasonably warm, if a trifle featureless, effect. There are various cast-in-place polyester floor coverings for kitchens and bathrooms, but as they have to be dealt with by a professional, they don't lend themselves to use by the home rebuilder.

Linoleum tiles come in a greater variety of styles, colors and textures than ever before, ranging from glossy supergraphic designs to textured Spanish "tiles." These are relatively easy to lay, but as mentioned before, linoleum laid in a continuous sheet roll is a project that the amateur builder should approach with caution. When any type of surfacing is applied in a single unbroken sheet, any small error along the way can spell disaster for the whole project.

Countertops

There are a number of popular countertops which perform much the same under use and differ mostly in their installation and visual effect. The two types found most often in kitchens are ceramic tile and laminated plastic veneer. Other possibilities include a new type of polyester "stone" tile, plastic "marble," linoleum and even fiber-glass-finished wood.

Whatever your choice turns out to be, it's a good idea to double-check the counter surface installation with the type of sink you prefer after reading over the sink installation section (if a new sink is to be put in). Not every kind of sink can be used with every type of countertop, and so it's best to investigate before committing yourself.

If you like laminated plastic veneer and want a well-finished look for the whole project, it's almost imperative to bring in a professional expert somewhere along the way. To save money, you can build the plywood base for the counter surface and then take it to a carpenter or sometimes an upholsterer to have it covered and edged. But check with the man before building the base; he'll show you exactly how he likes to handle corner joints if the counter is L-shaped, and he'll set you straight on other details.

As another alternative, you can build the plywood base in place and then call in a pro to surface it. You'll still save money.

There's not much trick to actually laying the surfaces, so you can try cutting a sheet of it to size and putting it down with the proper contact cement found at the lumberyard. The difficult part is making a nice edging, which is a little tough for a beginner with no special tools available. There are a number of vinyl-covered "wood" moldings that can be used to edge the surface, but that still doesn't help much if the sink is recessed below the countertop, necessitating a tightly curved edging piece around the sink. This is why we

64

recommend professional help when dealing with large laminated plastic countertops.

Ceramic tile, in general, is easier to install, is longer-wearing and usually presents an easier preparation job. The larger square tiles come with align-

When building a simple stained wood bar, decorative tiles can be inset into the surface to provide an attractive permanent hot plate.

65

ment tabs (that are later hidden under the grouting) to hold each tile a uniform distance from the adjoining tiles. The smaller tiles are laid in sheets with a backing that holds them in position so that you can put them down a square foot at a time.

The man-made, cast marble countertops are really better suited to bathroom use where the wear and tear is less and the surface areas are smaller. You can buy ready-made plastic counter-topping which is sold by the running foot, but the price is usually high and the choices are limited and generally look prefabricated.

If the countertop is for a little-used kitchen in a weekend house or an added apartment, where economy is of the essence, then sheet linoleum can be used. The installation of the sheet on a limited area such as a countertop doesn't present quite as much of a challenge as trying to lay a whole floor, and linoleum is reasonably durable used in this way.

You can also create interesting effects with a wooden countertop covered with a couple of layers of fiber glass. If you have even the slightest experience with the material, the actual process is easier than it may sound, but it takes a special kitchen to make a wooden counter seem natural.

Bear in mind when mulling over the possibilities that the color of the countertop may often do more than anything else to change the mood of a kitchen. So examine carefully the colors available in the type of counter you prefer; make sure you find one that will blend with the effect you're striving for. Step-by-step techniques for laying the counter surfaces discussed are to be found in the construction section.

Cabinets

There are a number of different levels on which you can approach the task of redoing the cabinets in the kitchen. You can leave them as they are and simply give them a new coat of paint, changing the hinges, handles and other hardware to help create a new look for the cabinetry. Or you can bring about a bigger change by taking off the cabinet doors and making new ones to fit in with the new look of the kitchen.

Of course, you can always rip the whole thing out and start over, but unless you have a definite, well-thought-out reason for radically changing the cabinet setup, it's rarely worth the trouble to start all over again. So much can be done to the doors and the hardware to change the look of things radically.

New door styles can vary all the way from natural or stained wood grain doors to complement a Danish modern approach, to raised-center panel doors with a "Regency" look. For a rougher, hand-hewn look, you may want to build recessed panel Spanish or Mediterranean stained doors with wrought iron hardware. It all depends on what you're looking for and how much time you can put into the project.

There are usually many obvious ways that extra shelving can be added in, around and between the cabinets to carry out a style theme as well as add greatly to the storage and display space in a kitchen. There is almost always an empty space over the refrigerator that is crying out for a shelf designed to help along the mood you like. Over a kitchen window is another opportunity for a shelf, or a cup and dish display board, or both. And even the end walls of the existing cabinets can provide a place to mount a small but handy shelf.

Inside the cabinets there are also a few opportunities to add helpful, if not quite so dramatic, shelving ideas to make your kitchen an easier place to work

The space above the refrigerator is almost universally left bare when the finish carpenters are through with a house. A shelf project like this can add both individuality and a great deal of functional area to a kitchen.

in. There is often a narrow broom closet somewhere in the room that can be made more functional as a "mini-pantry" for extra storage of canned goods. A few shelves added inside this sort of closet can help make shopping trips fewer and farther between.

Small shelves added between the regular food storage shelves in the cabinets can provide a place to put those small, hard-to-find items that you seem to spend a good deal of time looking for; they can be mounted on simple, triangular corbels or metal angle braces.

It's often worthwhile to move the mops and brooms out of the kitchen and fill the closet with shelves to create a handy "mini-pantry" which can cut down a good deal on the number of trips to the market.

Lighting

Most kitchens are lighted by somewhat institutional ceiling globes which usually don't do much for the personality of the room. To supplement these lights, or possibly replace them altogether, you can easily make up an unobtrusive indirect lighting system as shown in the illustration. By covering the lighting and its mounting, you can plug right into the existing lighting system and keep the wiring difficulties to a minimum. Or failing that, there is always the chance that you can replace the old globes with more imaginative ceiling-mounted lights to tie in with your style theme.

To get around the overpriced, flimsy and generally drab ceiling light fixtures found on the market, this builder simply ran fluorescent tubes (available at most used-lumber yards) along the ceiling and then suspended plastic grating, set in a simple wood frame, with short chains. The grate hides the tubes and creates a cheerful, indirect lighting effect.

69

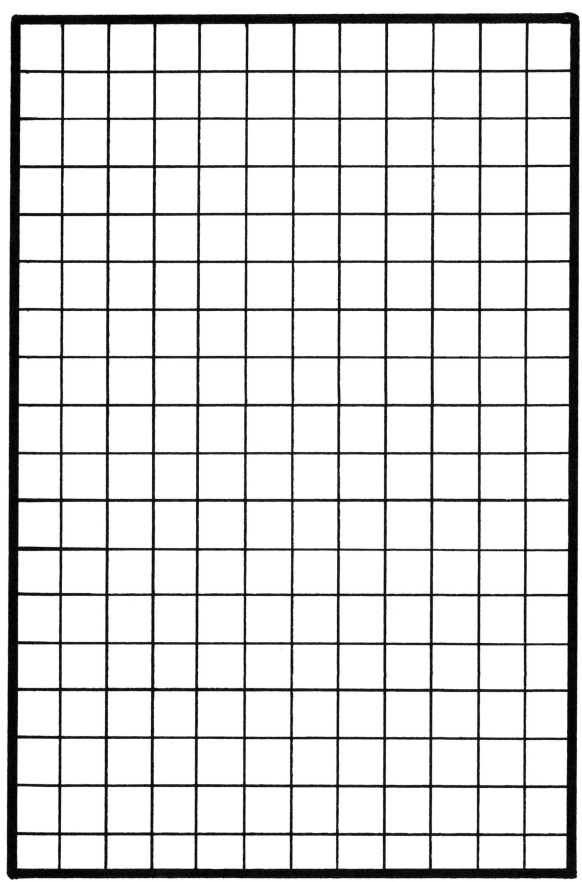

Floor Plan Design Grid. Each 1/2'' square equals one square foot.

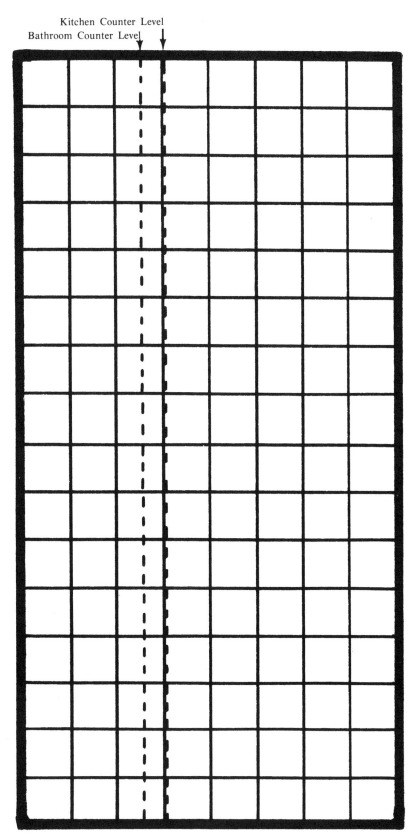

Kitchen Counter Level
Bathroom Counter Level

Wall Plan Design Grid. Each 1/2" square equals one square foot.

4

General Bathroom Ideas

The bathroom is where man traditionally greets the day's challenges and since those first crucial minutes of the day can do much to make or break the rest of it, it is well to plan pleasant surroundings to meet your eye—when it is finally propped open.

Despite the fact that much in a bathroom is dictated by the function of the fixtures, the room can still create the opportunities for a lot of designing fun.

If, on studying the traffic pattern of your house, you find that one bathroom is frequented by a significant majority of males, and that the reverse is true of the other bathroom, then you can begin to specialize—to create a mood for each that suits its clientele without having to deal with those annoying compromises that seem to crop up everywhere.

If the bathroom caters mostly to kids, you can pick up another theme, letting your creative ideas run a little wilder than usual within the privacy of the four walls. Whatever the mood, you can find it's much more fun to have a room that suits one specific outlook than to have to fit a theme into a multitude of different uses and points of view.

In an essentially feminine bathroom, you may want to create the feeling of an isolated sanctuary where a girl can commune at length with her hair without feeling as if she has happened into the men's locker room at the winter Olympics. On the other hand, a masculine bathroom may strive to provide a relaxed island of sanity where a fellow can dawdle over the shine of his shoes without feeling as if he's in an antique glassware shop. It can all help get things off on the right foot.

Wall covering has a lot to do with adapting the mood to masculine or feminine tastes. Traditionally, brighter colors and wallpapers have been more appreciated by women than men. And men, in turn, are supposed to respond more readily to wood tones and somber hues. We all know what a bunch of questionable nonsense all this really is. However, there's no disputing the fact that the associations are quite indelibly there. If you want a man's bathroom, you don't exactly line it with chandeliers and pink lace curtains—for what it's worth.

Now let's take a look at the ways typical bathrooms are arranged and the reasons why, and then we'll take each fixture, one by one, and figure out the options we have at each point.

To save money on the drainage system, most builders arrange the business end of the bathtub, the washbasin and the toilet along one side wall of the bathroom, with the tub farthest from the door. This provides a cheap enclosure for the tub on three sides and allows the inlet pipes, drain pipe and vent pipes to be contained within the side wall. It also makes the place look more than a little like a hospital wash-up room. However, the bathroom can retain all the sanitary qualities and still take on some fun—with a little help.

In a typical layout as described (and most other examples are simply slight variations on the theme), the lavatory basin is between the tub and the toilet, which is nearest to the door. Now the task at hand is to break up the monotony and to give as much feeling of separation of the different function areas as possible in the small space usually provided. Also on our list of objectives should be more closet space, more (or at least some) counter area and effective use of lights and mirrors.

Although it takes a major operation to switch the fixtures around (and it's hardly worth it in most cases), the sink can be moved a few inches without much trouble, and the tub and toilet can be modified in several ways to enhance their look and function.

Perhaps the one job that will do the most to achieve our list of objectives is a counter cabinet which can be built along the fixture wall with one or two floor-to-ceiling divider walls. In most bathrooms this will not only provide the needed separate privacy, counter space and added closet space, but it will also create a fertile layout for a host of different decorating themes. It will provide plenty of interesting opportunities for built-in indirect lighting and effective mirror mountings. And don't forget that divider walls actually make a room seem larger rather than smaller.

The skills needed to build such a counter-divider are simple, and the cost is very low—extremely low when you consider that in most cases such a conversion can either cover a worn out fixture that would otherwise have to be replaced, or draw attention away from it.

This counter-divider can be altered and varied endlessly to suit special cases. Since we've used this same basic layout as a basis for many different themes and moods, even with varying fixture positions and styles, there's a good chance such a project may solve many of your bathroom rebuilding problems. If not, you can still use the processes for modifying, moving, changing and generally refurbishing the fixtures in bringing your own layout ideas into play.

Now that we have a general idea of an answer that might work, let's take a look at the different options you can play around with for each of the fixtures and for the room itself.

73

Wall Treatments

In wall coverings you have a great choice, and even greater if you go outside what is usually associated with bathroom use. Bathrooms, do, admittedly, require special materials more than any other room to handle the variations in heat and moisture. However, some isolated materials not usually thought of for use in this room actually stand up better than many made specifically for the purpose. Whereas many species of paneling (and even pressed wood paneling with imitation wood grains) stand up remarkably well under the worst conditions, and even better with a couple of coats of water sealer, the officially sanctioned, widely used enamel-over-plaster combination is famous for its costly and ugly reactions to bathroom moisture conditions. Also, using acoustical tile on the ceiling, which is not recommended for installation in bathrooms, makes a surface that far outlasts its paint counterpart without forming—even in the worst conditions—the traditional brown moisture spots associated with overripe bathrooms.

Part of the mechanics of creating interest and life in a room is to use the unconventional and unexpected to inject a little fun into the living process. While we're thinking along unconventional lines, let's not forget the use of natural materials like rock and natural wood textures. They do a great job of relieving the dullness of a bathroom and are far easier to take care of than legend would have it. Admittedly, it's often difficult to work such materials into an old bathroom gracefully, but perhaps their use could be confined to planters and shelving and still give the same effect.

In the realm of conventional wall coverings, vinyl wallpaper stands up very well, and the new prepasted kind makes the job of installation easier. The most difficult task involved is picking the pattern you like from the thousands offered; hints for doing both the selecting and hanging of wallpaper can be found in the construction section.

Paneling has the advantage of being able to cover large holes without any extra work, and if you're moving the lighting around, it's easy to run the extension wires under the paneling. All types of paneling will stand up better if they're given a few coats of transparent water seal before the newly remodeled bathroom is actually used.

Painting is still the easiest way to give a wall a coat of color, but paint has no ability to cover large holes or hide wires or provide much interest for a surface. So it might be easier in the long run, depending on the condition of the walls, to use a paper or wood covering. Because bathrooms need at least a semigloss paint surface, to permit cleaning, the spackling job to fill in cracks and holes has to be pretty smooth in order for the coat of paint to be an improvement over the old wall surfaces. With gloss paint you have brush and roller strokes to contend with as well; consequently, you may want to think twice about using paint over a large area in the bathroom. The practices for painting as well as paneling can be found in the construction section.

Another way to add interest to the room is to use old, weathered lumber.

74

We've seen entire walls that were covered with boards taken from a barn being torn down. Even weathered fruit packing boxes can be dismantled and used to cover a special interest area. Another effect is created by sanding weathered lumber lightly to bring out the highlights, and then sealing or varnishing it to bring up the color. With antique tools added, the whole effect can get pretty rustic in a hurry.

In this case the divider wall forms the medicine cabinet. The shuttered side swings open to expose the wall frame shelving.

Flooring

Flooring is another subject that calls for a little original thinking. Just a few years back, no professional in his right mind would have risked his reputation by recommending carpeting in a bathroom or kitchen. But with the advent of new materials, the use has spread until it is finally becoming the official thing to suggest. It may be a good thing too, for a cold, hard, waxed surface is not the most comfortable thing to walk on in the early morning.

You can buy special bathroom carpeting that comes in various precut sizes, all wrapped up in neat packages. And since the bathroom area is usually fairly small, you can buy remnants of very good quality carpeting at surprisingly low cost. This may be the solution if you have an unusual color combination you are working with, since the prepackaged carpeting comes in standard shades and textures. Again, since the area to be covered is generally not very large, it isn't necessary to tack the carpet down except perhaps at the door. This means you can take the carpet out easily to clean it.

You can replace the linoleum, that's more than likely ready for a change, but you may just be re-creating a situation in which water gets trapped under the "waterproof" surface and rots out the wood. Sheet linoleum is devilishly hard for an amateur to contend with, and you're better off to stick with the squares if you want linoleum at all.

There are waterproof cork tiles that might create an interesting effect in a bathroom. The floor can also be covered with ceramic tile to match other tile in the room, but the glue will bond only on a solid base. You can even carry out a natural wood sauna bath motif with a wood-finish grating over the floor.

Windows and Indoor-Outdoor Treatments

Giving interest to twentieth-century windows can be a challenge. In ready-made windows for bathrooms, the field we have to choose from is pretty meager. There's the old style opaque, wood frame transom window; the extruded sliding glass institutional window; and the drafty louver window. On viewing the contenders, you may want to take out the window altogether and put in a vent fan. But if you want the natural light, maybe we can think of a variation or combination that will do the trick without too much pain.

It's generally accepted that even aluminum windows are more satisfactory than the transom lean-out-at-the-top type. So if you don't balk at the look of the aluminum beauties, then it's easy to take out the transom and mount a slider or louver in its place after a little trimming and cutting. Another answer is to build a 1'' x 6'' wood box framework to just fit the opening. Then fill the center with small rectangular panes of all sorts of opaque glass textures mounted in a wood framing, with a panel of short louvers included to provide adequate venting. Still another idea is to run a framing of wood molding around the window to relieve the utilitarian drabness of metal window frames.

The indoor-outdoor look of a small, fenced garden seen through a clear glass window is another approach to take. With adequate provision for privacy in the form of fencing, an opaque (or "obscure glass" as it's known in the trades) window can be replaced with clear glass, or a new window can even be cut to provide a striking inside-outside look for the bathroom. These small gardens are the perfect place for using interesting natural materials in the

There are times when you can bring nature right in with you. In this case mirrors double the jungle effect.

form of rock or brick planters which can provide a bright splash of live color from plants and flowers.

The ultimate indoor-outdoor look that we've encountered was one in which the lawn came in through French doors and provided a portion of the bathroom floor covering. Of course, you may not want to go this far, but it does show what can be done to good effect, once you set your mind to looking for interesting new answers to monotonous old problems.

In this bathroom simple, inexpensive light mounts have been covered with a sheet of white translucent plastic to create an attractive indirect light. Extruded aluminum "J-bars," normally used to support mirrors, form the top edges for the plastic.

78

Lighting and Mirrors

Most old bathrooms have one adequate, but not necessarily pleasing, light over the one small mirror cabinet. At reasonable cost, and with a little of your time, you can replace this uninspired combination with a good plate glass mirror, a large (nonrusting) wooden cabinet made to your own needs, and a complete indirect lighting system. Steps for making typical examples follow in

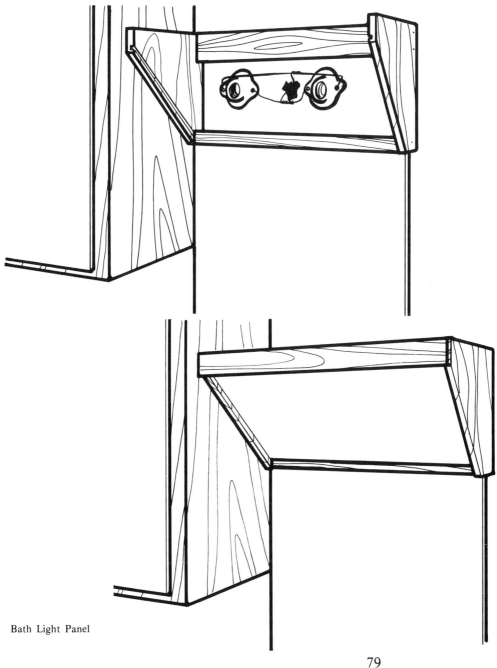

Bath Light Panel

Indirect lighting, created by setting wide, opaque glass louvers in a simple notched-end frame, can provide a warm, inviting effect at a fraction of the cost of store-bought fixtures. Both bulb sockets and louvers can usually be found at house-wrecking yards.

chapter 19, as well as directions for installing mirrors. However, if you haven't the time or desire to set up indirect lighting, you might try looking at lamps, especially ceiling and wall lamps, which are not usually thought of for bathroom use, to create a little interest. Perhaps the lighting could be built around mementos serving as the nucleus of a decorating theme. Special-interest ideas for lights abound, like antique car lamps, boat lights, etc., which can easily be adapted to a standard light socket.

Toilets

The first fixture we meet on entering the bathroom is usually the toilet. Now this cornerstone of modern civilization, admirable though it may be in many ways, is fairly inflexible as a tool of decorative self-expression. True, some have lower water tanks than others, and a few eccentrics are even wall-mounted; but by and large, they are all the same, despite cosmetic variations and individual detail differences in their innards.

To move a toilet even a few meager inches involves all the red tape of heavy plumbing. So the best that can be done with a toilet that has seen better days is to cover up as much of it as possible (the tank) with cabinetry or replace it altogether, or both. These are simple jobs and new toilets, compared to most plumbing articles, are a surprisingly good buy, considering what you get for your money. Remember, when planning a narrow cabinet shelf which will cover the tank and tie the fixture into the rest of the counter, that there must be easy access to the insides of the tank, or you'll be in for trouble. A removable top is the obvious answer. Also, there are inexpensive push button units on the market to replace the toilet's traditional trip lever; these can bring the control out through the front of the cabinetry. Details are in the construction section, of course.

Sinks

The next piece of porcelain we come to is the lavatory sink. Although the models used in most mass-built houses are usually simple wall-mounted styles, sinks come in every shape, mounting and color. No other fixture in plumbing changes quite so radically with the tides of plumbing fashion as the sink, and it's usually the sink that first tells you how old the rest of the plumbing in the room is. If your existing sink is in good shape, and is a simple wall-mounted edition without too much baroque ornamentation, then you may want to keep it and blend it into the countertop design. If it could be mounted a few inches to one side or the other to create a better counter space layout, this, too, can be arranged with very little trouble. The steps for such a project are shown in the construction section.

If the sink is a little beyond its prime, both in looks and condition, it may be a good time to replace it with an oval counter-mounted species that is inexpensive (as sinks go) and can blend in pleasingly with a great variety of decorative styles. These come in all degrees of finery and mounting complexity to suit your fancy. Some mount under the counter material; some are flush with the counter, using a stainless steel mounting ring around the sides; and some sit down over a hole cut in the countertop. The simplest is this last style, which mounts with ease on any counter material. The cheapest is usually the ring type, made of stamped steel. If you're looking for anything but an economy measure, this is not the answer, and by the time you buy the stainless steel ring (which is fabulously overpriced in most cases), the sink will end up

This toilet tank has been covered with a planter base. The tops of such covers must be easily removable to allow access to the tank valve.

costing as much as the porcelain or cast-iron model. The counter bottom-mounted styles have the dubious distinction of requiring a finished counter edge around the sides. This isn't too hard if you decide to use a professionally finished plastic laminated counter surface, but it can mean trouble if you want to save money by finishing the countertop yourself. Try to find a sink that can be mounted over the counter finish around the sinkhole. In some cases sinks made to be mounted under the counter edge can actually be mounted over it. So the best course is to ask to see all the sinks available, and then decide for yourself if they can be mounted on top of the counter surface. If the edge of the mounting lip is glazed like the rest of the sink, and the bottom of the lip is fairly flat, then the sink can be used as is. If you can't find anything but a sink with an unglazed mounting lip, you can sometimes put a coating of tub caulk around the edge of the lip to blend it into the countertop.

If you can find a large supplier, or a used fixture yard, you may often come across new "seconds" which have a tiny defect that won't hurt the running of them and may save you twenty or thirty percent. Even when buying new, full-priced items from reputable dealers, check your fixtures before leaving the store. With sinks in particular, make certain the mounting surface for the drain on the bottom around the drain hole is flat. This seems to be the area that most manufacturers have problems with, and it's where a leak is likely to develop. Look over the surface finish carefully for holes and cracks that might have slipped by.

Countertops and Counter Cabinets

With countertops you also have several ways to go. You can buy ready-made vanity cabinets with counters and sinks attached. But as you may have guessed, they'll cost you a pretty penny, and they really don't provide much counter space or any division of functional areas. Or you can buy presurfaced laminated plastic counters to be cut and fitted onto your own framework. Again, it costs a bit. Another way is to build the counter cabinet box so that the top can be removed and taken to a cabinet or furniture finishing shop to be covered with the laminated plastic veneer of your choice. Or, so long as we're on the plastic bit, you can cover the counter surface yourself with the veneer (which is the simple part of the job). Then instead of trying to get a professional edge look, which takes a bit of experience and special tools, cover the edging with wood moldings which can be either easily made on a table saw or adapted from ready-made strips.

In place of plastic you can tile the counter, a reasonably simple affair if problem areas are avoided in the original planning. Still another way is to make a finished wood counter of your favorite grain and cover this with fiber glass.

So far as the framework and sides of the counter cabinet (as well as the divider walls) go, we show the steps for a typical installation in the construction section; these steps can be modified or used as is, according to your needs.

Sinks which mount on top of the counter surface are easiest to work with. No trim edge is needed on the counter surface, and mounting is simple.

Tub Enclosures and Showers

Next comes the bathtub. Because bathtubs are reasonably anonymous things, as fixtures go, and because they are a bit of a job to replace (as well as expensive), it may be best to try to hide the drawbacks and make the best of the one you have—unless you're considering a major change in fixture color, or a conversion to a shower enclosure. There are various ways to cover up and draw attention away from these flaws, and they are a lot cheaper and more fun than spending time and money to replace a tub, only to end up with basically the same concept you started with.

If the tub has no provision for a shower, putting one in is a simple job that can add more versatility to a bathroom per dollar than any other project. The plumbing can be changed with a simple flexible attachment that screws into the inlet spout pipe. And there are a number of effective, simple, inexpensive ways to waterproof the surrounding walls. You can choose from waterproof sheets of "tile" or marbleized material that is put up like wood paneling, ready-spaced miniature ceramic tiling that goes on in one-foot squares or standard four-inch-square tiles with built-in spacers on the edges. All are fairly simple techniques that are covered in the construction section.

The style of tub enclosures can do much to set the mood of a bathroom as well as cover up a worn tub. An interesting curtain, with an imaginative mounting to create the effect of an enclosed, separate bath area, might be worth the money to update a dull tub arrangement.

Sliding glass tub enclosures are an answer that can completely shut off the tub area in a half hour's work. The installation is simple, once you know a couple of basic principles, and is covered in the construction section too. Just make certain you're getting tempered glass or wire-glass, which is mandatory in many areas (and a good idea anywhere).

If you're confronted with a dull bath layout that needs more than a face-lifting (and provided you have the proper ambition, of course), you can go in for radical changes. Give a new look to the bathroom, update its concept and create a great deal more closet room for your house by converting the old bathtub arrangement to a shower enclosure with a linen closet or possibly a new dressing room/make-up area filling the floor space gained in the conversion.

The job will take more than a spare Saturday afternoon, of course, but the cost will probably be less than you expect, and the results will make a whole new room of it. In a typical layout the project will involve taking out the old tub, installing shower flooring, building the enclosing walls, having the lead-in and drainage pipes changed, and tiling and installing a shower door. After that, the painting, papering or paneling and the installation of dressing table counters or storage shelves and closet doors are your own choices.

You'll be required to have some of the work done by professionals in most areas, and you may want to have some of the rest of the work done by pros as well; but just so you'll understand what needs to be done, we'll explain in the construction section the steps taken to build such an enclosure.

Before you think you're through giving the room your best, take another look around at all the components and details for some forgotten chance to convey the mood you want to get. Even door knobs and cabinet handles can provide a chance to give an impression, like a rustic lever latch instead of a conventional chrome door knob if you want a rural look; or maybe a cabin latch from a boat for a door knob and cleats for drawer pulls. The same principle goes for towel bars, clothes hooks, soap dishes and the like. Search through your trophies and curios for something unlikely, such as antlers for hooks or seashells for soap dishes, that would work just as well as those normally used and create a little variety at the same time. It takes a little looking around, just as anything special takes a little extra time and effort but not necessarily more money.

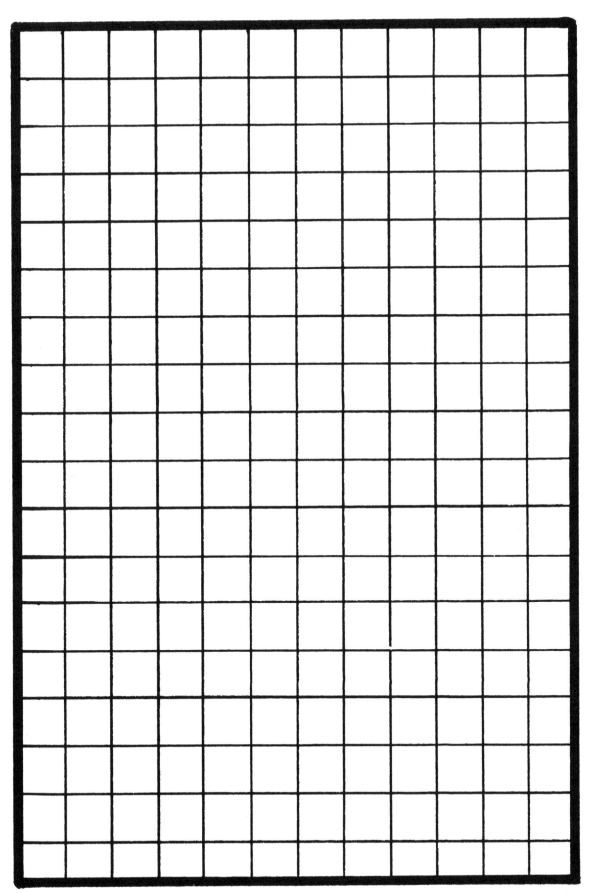

Floor Plan Design Grid. Each 1/2" square equals one square foot.

Kitchen Counter Level
Bathroom Counter Level

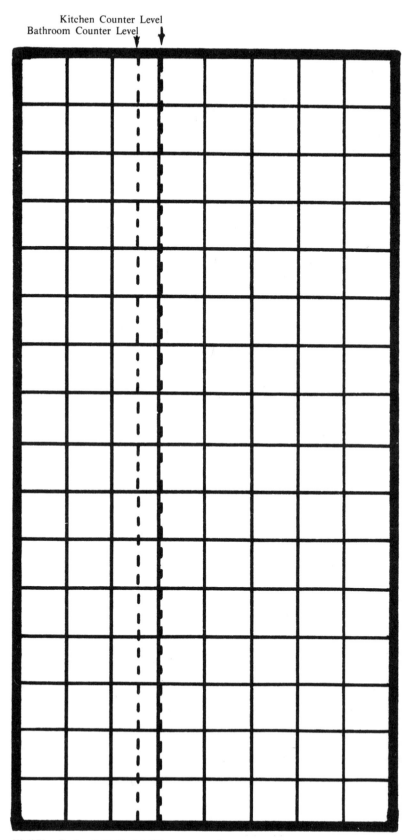

Wall Plan Design Grid. Each 1/2" square equals one square foot.

Cut-Out Fixtures.

89

5

General Bedroom Ideas

In many houses the bedrooms represent a great amount of wasted floor space. It's not that we have anything against bedrooms as a class, but the fact remains that they take up a large proportion of the house. They aren't generally used during the daylight hours as much as they might be, and when they are used at night, nobody sees much of them anyway. When you're working with an already limited amount of floor area, this can be a great waste of your house's potential.

In days gone by, bedrooms were often personal work areas where one could spend some time getting caught up on his writing or reading. The actual bedding area amounted to only a small, shelflike bed-closet set into one wall where you could catch a few winks when the attention began to wander.

Even in some modern bachelor diggings the bed can disappear almost entirely, being replaced by work areas, bookcases, music paraphernalia or even gym equipment. Of course, the confirmed bachelor is a special case, and we've seen things get to the point where one bedroom is completely overwhelmed by a floor-to-ceiling amplifier with thirty-eight speakers; in another room a vintage race car may be undergoing restoration. But then, we don't pretend that this is everybody's cup of tea.

The opposite end of the scale isn't much more sensible, either. In a typical master bedroom, a huge bed dominates all, sitting right in the center of the room, covering substantial square yardage of carpeting that never gets walked on.

To make things a little more useful, you may want to think about rearranging the layout to provide enough room for a small, personal work area or studio. A bedroom can provide a good place to get away from the distracting world so you can concentrate on a relaxing interest such as sewing, needlepoint, music, building live steam engines, or whatever moves you. Adding a special-use area to a bedroom can not only create an interesting, purposeful look for the design of the room, it can also help add a little extra something to your life by providing a comfortable place to follow a hobby.

If you don't seem to have any creative pursuits to keep you busy, perhaps a favorite sport or collecting hobby can be worked into the bedroom layout to give you a place to wax your skis, polish newly found antiques or mount butterflies in restful seclusion. We've even seen a bedroom set up for watching the stock-market returns on a special TV station—with all the necessary deep leather chairs, telephones, coffeemakers and aspirin within easy reach. Whatever the interest, a bedroom with special-use areas can add to the potential of a house, while taking the load off the living room, which often has to try to fulfill these functions without the needed seclusion.

Children's bedrooms are another special case. To a child, his bedroom (even if shared) can actually become a house within a house—a shelter from the adult world where his own dictates can prevail for once. This doesn't mean he can pour paint on the rug or shoot out the windows, of course, but within reason the child should be able to see his mark in the decoration of the room.

What appears to be clutter to the adult eye is often simply a group of little interest areas to a kid. Each square foot of a work table or floor isn't just a small corner of the house to a child (who spends many hours getting to know every inch of his diggings), but rather a large proportion of his own miniature world, built around the imaginative activities of his toys and projects. So it may be a good idea to think twice before inflicting any sort of clutter-free, clean-line design on the world of a child, for clutter can sometimes be a fertile source of new ideas and interests to a child's mind. It's always a little pitiful to see a hospital-neat, carefully arranged and highly decorated child's room which was created solely to please the eye of the overseeing adult.

You can spend as much as you like on fancy beds and cute-as-pie lamps. But what a child would probably appreciate more is a good carpet to work on and an intriguing layout with all sorts of little corners, benches, cubbyholes, lofts and shelters. A rich, varied background to serve as a stimulus for imaginative play may be what a child would like more than fairy-tale wallpaper.

The more the child or children in question can be consulted on the building of their room, the more it will become a special place to them. Things like fabric-covered pinup boards where they can put up a constantly changing display of their own favorite cutouts from magazines can add a personal touch. Even in choosing the basic colors for the rooms, try to get a second opinion from the kids. And don't be surprised if they choose a subtle blending of warm, earthy colors instead of the garish primary colors that remind adults of the vividness of natural colors during childhood.

Most toys are made to sell to adults, and sometimes decorators will try to carry the same colors and themes into a child's room—with the result that it may please the adult but not necessarily the child. We've tested the theory in practice in a number of different ways, and we're convinced that kids like warm, subtle, natural colors far better than garishly bright, unmixed primary hues. Again, this touches on the realm of personal preference and your children may not feel this way about colors. The main thing is to give them a say in the planning of their domain.

Dressers, wall shelves and lighting can sometimes be built into one project to keep the floor of a child's room cleared for action. In this case the unit is used to split an existing room into two bedrooms, providing shelf space for both rooms. What is shelf area in this view is flat, graphic display space on the other side, and vice versa.

On the opposite side, the pattern of flat display areas and shelving is reversed.

A kid's room is a natural place for built-in storage/work areas, bed/storage areas and flexible multiuse furniture projects. Although we haven't recommended flexible shelving and foldaway furniture for other areas of the house (because they tend to be installed one way and then left that way permanently), the many different activities that take place in a child's room may make flexible furniture worthwhile. Kids often have relatively short bursts of intense interest, and the more a room can be changed to accommodate these periods of feverish activity, the more lasting appeal it can have. The beauty about many built-ins is that they can make store-bought furniture unnecessary, thereby saving on the costs of the materials to create a really individual room.

Generally, the choices open to us in rebuilding a bedroom are much the same ones that we found in the living room section, with a little more emphasis on the economical (if no special-interest use can be found to augment the usually small amount of waking time spent in an adult's bedroom).

Wall Covering Choices

The flat finish latex paints are well suited to bedroom use, of course, with semigloss needed only for trim and doors. Paint is inexpensive and easy to apply but still doesn't create very dramatic effects and has to be renewed every few years.

93

Paneling is a natural for bedrooms because of its warm effect and long life as a wall covering; and once it's up, you can pretty well forget about maintenance. Since carpet, curtain and bedspread fabrics cover a large area of what you see in a bedroom, and can provide an easy way to get dramatic color effects, it's often a good idea to go easy on the wall coverings in a bedroom. By sticking to the simple grains found in inexpensive paneling, you can avoid creating too many intricate surface patterns in one small room and still retain the durability and warmth of wood paneling (saving yourself a bundle at the same time).

The same generally goes for wallpaper in a bedroom, although the situation is slightly different. Because wallpaper is an image pattern much like bedspread and curtain fabrics, you can have either an interesting wallpaper with a complementary but not too distracting curtain and spread combination, or you can reverse it and use intricate curtain and bedspread fabrics with a subdued wallpaper. There are also many wallpapers with matching or

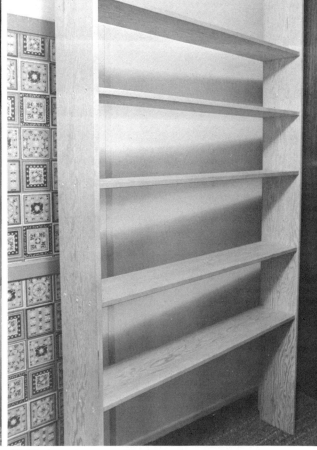

(1) A typical, bare and unexciting corner about which the less said, the better.

(2) Work under way. Shelving units should be assembled a little removed from the eventual position to allow screws to be sunk from the back side.

94

complementary fabrics available which can work together to provide a nicely integrated touch in the room. Since there are no special conditions to contend with, as there are in kitchens and bathrooms, you can use practically any kind of paper and pattern you like.

It's our guess that simple, cheerful and colorful wall coverings may be better suited to bedrooms than dramatically inventive textures such as shingles and rocks. The latter tend to make a room more exciting rather than

(3) Shelves assembled and fastened in position with countersink holes plugged and edges sanded and ready for staining. The legs of the child's work table are hinged at the top, allowing them to swing out of the way when the tabletop is folded down into the shelf front.

95

a calm, relaxing sanctuary where you can knit the raveled sleeve. In a bedroom a person is at the mercy of the design style as he lies in quiet contemplation of the ceiling and walls before hitting the deck to start the day. For that reason we recommend something not too overwhelming, yet easy to live with, in the way of a design style. But, again, it all depends on the mood you're after.

Flooring

Flooring is extremely important in children's rooms, less so in other bedrooms. An inviting carpet can make a child's room a great place to play, and the amount of hours spent in the room will skyrocket amazingly after a fresh, colorful carpeting is laid. For use in children's rooms, the carpeting need not be expensive, and a braided or short-pile rug will do the job nicely. Again, the indoor-outdoor type of carpeting does not stand up very well in this sort of use. A multicolored pattern is best to hide the inevitable spills that will eventually dot the surface of the carpet no matter how you warn against it.

In master bedrooms the traffic is light compared to other areas in the house, and you may be able to use a type of carpeting in this room that would not stand the wear and tear in a kitchen or bathroom. Since the areas are much larger (with a good deal of it covered by beds and dressers), it may be excusable to use a more economy-minded carpet here.

Another way to get around the wasted carpet in a master bedroom is to use colorful area rugs over the hardwood floors. You may also want to think about putting something other than carpeting on the floor in the special interest areas of the bedroom. If you're going to be doing any "messy" creating, such as painting or refinishing antiques, cork or linoleum tiles would work well.

Curtains

Curtains and valance boards seem to be an important part of a bedroom. Since they can work with the bedding fabrics to create much of the finished effect of the room, you may want to spend the effort and money you saved in floor and wall coverings to add interest in this direction.

As we mentioned before, if you're using wallpaper, there are often matching fabrics available that work well, either as a cover for valance boards or in the curtains themselves. Of course, if you choose a particularly rich, impressive curtain material, you may want to mount it on a more ornate, formal antique curtain rod arrangement. If an intricate wall or curtain pattern is used, you may choose to cover up the "busyness" of the folds at the top of the curtains with a simple valance board.

Built-In Furniture

Built-ins are almost as well suited to adults' bedrooms as they are to children's. In many cases a wall can be covered with a built-in closet that will also create a work or dressing table area to one side, with a well-placed divider wall or two. Details for a sample of such a project are found in the Built-in

96

When a spare room or garage is to be converted into a bedroom, the first project is to build new closet space. This example, described in the construction section, can be paneled, covered with drywall to be painted, or covered with plywood to be plastered or papered.

portion of the construction section. Other built-in possibilities to look over include bookshelf headboards, work bench or dressing table/storage areas, and a four-poster canopy to form the focal point for the room (if the bed is to be retained as the center of interest for the room after all).

The range of possibilities for built-ins in children's rooms is endless. All that's needed is a little imagination.

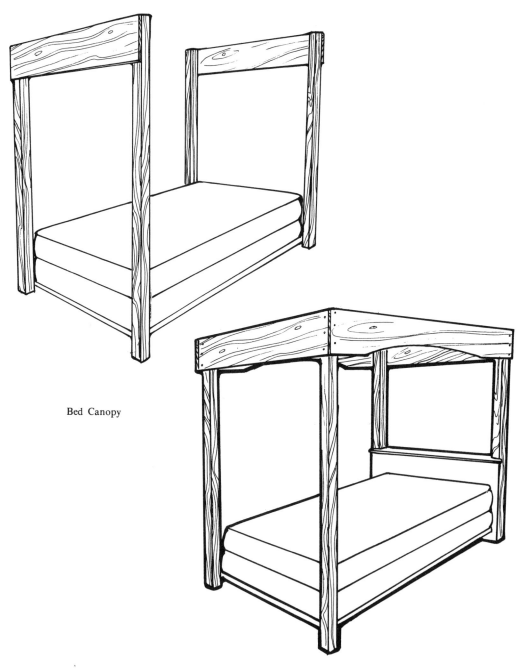

Bed Canopy

General Bedroom Ideas

The things lacking in almost all kids' rooms are the things they seem to need the most: shelves. Shelves serve endless functions—they help keep the mess off the floor; they add greatly to the storage space of the room; and they add a lot of interest and life in the form of display areas for colorful toys and games. The wall component shelves with fold-up work table, as shown in the illustrations, are a very handy addition to a child's room.

Lots of built-in shelves, together with a warm combination of carpeting and paneling, add up to an inviting child's room, suitable for all sorts of play.

A combination bed-desk-closet along one wall, leaving the rest of the room free for play activities, might work well. This sort of project lends itself to various design themes such as a Tyrolean Alps "Heidi" motif, perhaps with a loft above the bed, or possibly a rustic "bunkhouse" effect.

Windows

If you're more ambitious than some, you may think about changing the style of the windows themselves if they appear particularly drab and lifeless to you. In this case it's a good idea to build your project around what you can find as a substitute. A house-wrecking yard usually has the most varied and least expensive selection of interesting window substitutes. Perhaps a clever window box/reading seat combination can add enough interest to the window arrangement to draw attention away from its bad points. And there is always the possibility of running a more appealing wood framing around the existing metal frame if an extruded metal window is the source of the starkness. It's a good idea to make the ornamental wood framing easily removable, however, to keep it from blocking access when new glass has to be installed.

A much more involved window treatment project would be some sort of indoor-outdoor effect—perhaps replacing the window with a sliding glass door leading out to a small, fenced-in patio where you can commune with nature.

6

Ideas for MultiUse Rooms

There is a class made up of several different types of rooms which are quite unlike each other in appearance but fall into the same category because of the role they play in the activities of the household: the special-purpose rooms.

These can range all the way from the rather formal trophy rooms, bars, libraries and studies to the all-purpose workshop-party room and ping-pong salon (with the model train hung from the ceiling).

The one thing they all have in common is that they're not absolutely essential to human survival in a biological sense—and as such, are all generally dedicated to favorite leisure pastimes. Whether it's because you have a ready-made, built-in design theme to work from or because the whole execution of such a room is generally much more lighthearted than the rest of the house, the designing and building can be a good deal of fun for all involved.

More often than not, these dens, playrooms, family rooms or whatever you want to call them are generally so personal and informally attractive that everyone invariably ends up spending more time in this room, sitting on discarded couches and old car seats, than in their carefully arranged living rooms that cost so much to furnish. There may be a lesson in there someplace for those who spend a lot of time rebuilding a house.

No matter what decorative moods are used in the rest of the house, in the family, trophy or game room the key word is personal preference. The dictates of your family's own active interests are the only criteria for an attractive special-use room. As the name implies, it's a room to serve your leisure activities, regardless of the latest correct decorating rules or the impression it makes on the neighbors—whether you make yours a cozy, contemplative spot in which to delve into a good book amid your life's trophies, or a work or play area to make your hobbies or sports possible.

Of course, when we speak of trophies, we don't limit them to the silver or brass variety. A good trophy room can contain any favorite objects that remind you of past triumphs and good times—sporting equipment, blow-ups of your favorite sporting scenes, favorite photos, old guns, musical instruments, ship models or whatever you happen to like.

If you have an extra TV, this is the obvious room to store it so you can watch that old thriller free from the fear of interruption by the normal course of things. This type of room lends itself equally well to the needs of the man who finds he can't quite get all that Beethoven has to offer when the little ones decide to restage the Indian wars.

If it's this type of quiet, contemplative refuge room that you're looking for, then a small, dark, cozy place may be the answer. Since the general idea behind such a den or study is to provide a relaxed, secluded sanctum sanc-

You never know where you might run across a handy piece of fun furniture for a playroom. An old wooden icebox found in a junk shop can be stripped down to bare wood and then stained to create a handsome place to store records and tapes.

In a studio-workroom the shelves can get pretty rough treatment, depending on your hobby. If so, there's little reason to spend a lot of money on the woodwork. This unit makes use of floor-to-ceiling 2" x 4" uprights to steady the actual shelves formed by old packing crates and fruit boxes.

torum, the decorative style should do everything it can to carry out this theme. Subdued carpeting, warm dark paneling and deep leather chairs (not to speak of brandy snifters) are brought to mind. Add to this some good old books you like, a few bits of memorabilia (that no one realizes the importance of) to make you feel comfortably at home, and you're all set.

On the other hand, if your interests lie along more active lines, including such favorite indoor sports as painting, sewing, potting, sculpting, model building, collecting, woodworking or other innocent pursuits, then what you'll be looking for is a clean, well-lighted place with plenty of fresh air, windows, work benches and shelving space.

The furniture in such a studio room can be almost entirely built-in with only an occasional store-bought stool or chair to fill out what you'll need. Of course, the woodwork in a workroom gets pretty rough treatment, so the shelves and benches can be built out of inexpensive woods and finished simply.

One of the most important features of a good studio room is a well-thought-out lighting system. When getting the details of any creative project just right, the eyes get quite a workout, and it helps if the maximum amount of overhead lighting and possibly even skylights can be worked into the basic layout. As most people know, fluorescent lights (which are the most likely candidate for lighting such a room) flicker on and off sixty times a second. Although these

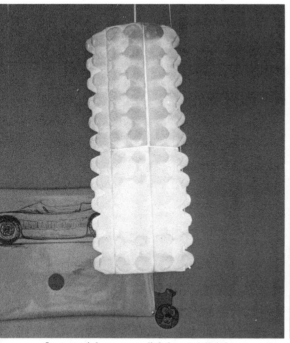

In a special-use room lighthearted lighting may do the job as well as or better than ready-made units. This specimen is fairly easy to figure out, being made of plastic egg crates; but the lighting effect is remarkably inviting.

In playrooms it's ingenuity that has to save the day when the budget is a bit on the thin side. Here the necessity to change the harsh light of a ceiling bulb led to the use of paper cups stapled together to create a soft, indirect light.

lights are cool and cheap to run, they should be used *along with* standard incandescent lights, or the flickering can produce bad eyestrain when doing close work.

With a little imagination the very tools and work samples of your hobby can provide all the decoration you need to make a studio interesting—while the amenities such as floor and wall coverings take a back seat to the more functional features. If your activities take a lot of standing up, you may want to find an old rug that will ease the foot strain, for it's important to the success of your hobby to have a work area that caters to your creature comforts. This may not mean a luxurious layout in many cases—just a close following of your personal preferences.

Playrooms are another type that falls into this functional-emphasis category. Since the role of such rooms is to provide a place to play a number of different games, in most cases the things to strive for are a maximum of usable floor space and a flexible basic layout. To get enough square footage without eating into the functions of the house, the usual candidate for conversion into a playroom is a basement or garage—although the more ambitious may want to investigate the possibility of building a simple room addition to make the playroom just the way they want it.

The decor, of course, is usually pretty informal, but this is no excuse to forget the inclusion of some attractive color and warmth in the look of the room. In fact, a playroom is a good place to try out your wilder ideas if you happen to have a yen to follow the whimsical approach. Or you may want a seasonal sort of style that is easy to create and easy to rip out when you get tired of it. At any rate, flexibility is the key word.

Wall Treatments

Wall coverings should be cheap and rugged. A constantly changing graphic display may be seen on the walls much of the time, so the wall finish should blend in nicely with tack and dart holes. In fact, making a special fabric-over-cork wall for a changing display of graphic decorations like posters and blowups to match the current interest of the room may be a good way to prolong the life of the other walls.

Paneling is an obvious choice, if the budget can take it, for a nonessential room such as this. There are several types of very inexpensive paneling that would work out well in this sort of area. All special interest wall textures should be checked for durability before use. If the wall won't stand up well when fallen against or doesn't resist the butt of a pool cue every so often, then better think about something else. A playroom wall will go through every manner of abrasion and impact test before its time is up.

Flooring

Carpeting is nice and warm, but it may be a waste to lay it in extremely high-use areas such as under the ends of a Ping-Pong table. Cork tiles create a warm and slightly soft floor surface at a reasonable price, as does linoleum in tile form. But since the wear and tear is high, and the premium on super-finished decorative style in flooring low, the best idea may be to make use of what slab or wood floor is already there. Area rugs can be included in the places that could make use of a softer, warmer floor covering. Keep an eye on the newspaper ads—it may be that you can pick up a bargain in the way of discontinued styles of flooring or carpet remnants that will make it possible for you to cover the floor the way you'd like to.

Here a hidden-away area in an attic has been opened up to create a special loft, just for kids. Like a treehouse, the hideaway loft provides an all-important place to get away from it all (but staying close enough to hear the dinner gong).

Ideas for Multiuse Rooms

Built-In Couch

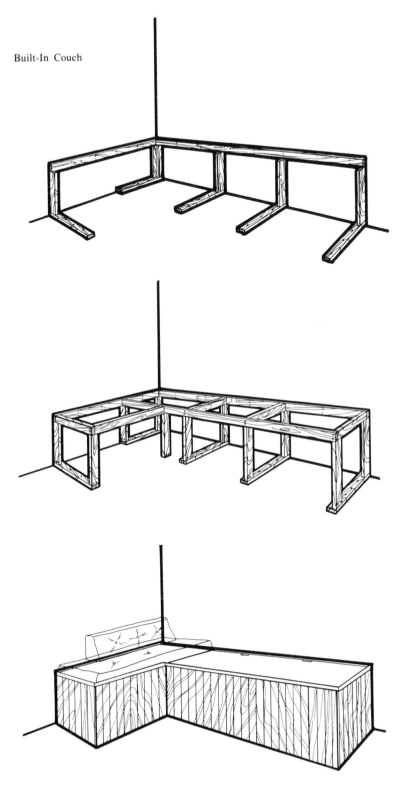

In this wall component, drawers have been included with the shelving to provide added versatility.

Ideas for Multiuse Rooms

Built-In Workbench

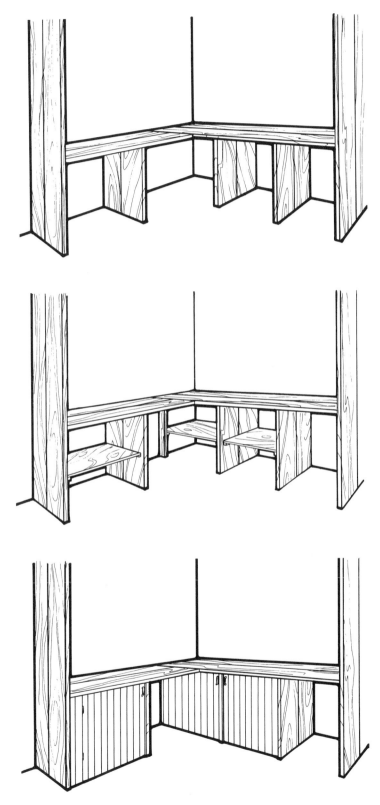

Built-Ins

Playrooms lend themselves well to built-in couches with storage space beneath the pads for out-of-season sporting equipment and such. As these couches follow the periphery of the room in most cases, you can use them to provide ample seating area and storage space while keeping almost all of the usable floor area open to suggestions. Wall component shelf units are just the thing to create a place for record players, tools and current sporting equipment in a remarkably small area. To cut costs, a cheaper grade of economical wood can be used and then painted interesting colors.

It's often the case that an occasional furnace or drain pipe will have to be included in with the rest of the decorative details of the room. When this happens, the first impulse is to cover up the offender with some hopeful form of boxing-in. Before any great amount of effort is expended on a cosmetic cover-up, perhaps you should think about ways that the piece of plumbing or ventilation itself can be adorned to form part of the background of the room.

Sometimes with an imaginative bit of painting, a pedestrian piece of functionality can be given a whimsical touch that makes it fit right into the lighthearted, form-follows-function mood of the room. We've even seen heavy wiring lines turned into grapevines that somehow mysteriously ended up growing in the room after a little creative painting and the addition of plastic leaves. It didn't fool anybody, but it covered up an ugly spot with a bit of fun.

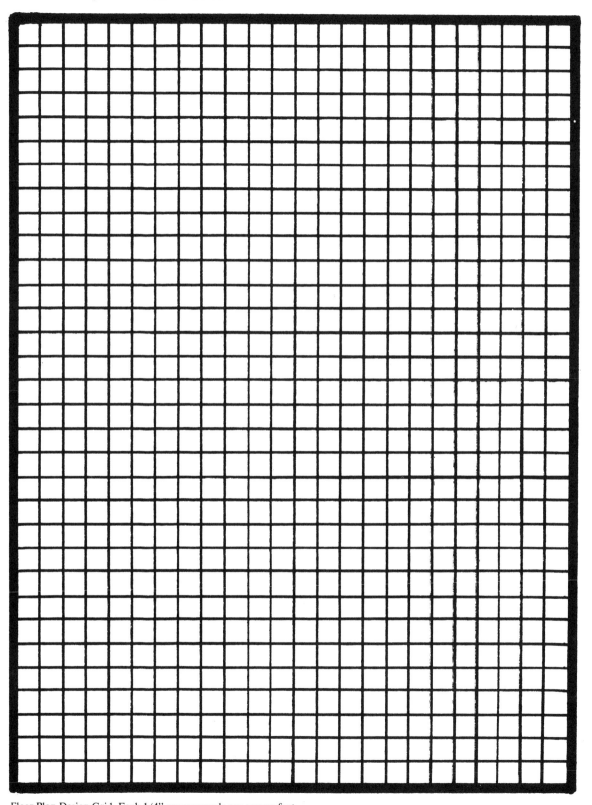

Floor Plan Design Grid. Each 1/4" square equals one square foot.

7

Painting

The first step in painting a room is to select the color, type and brand of paint, as we've discussed in the general section. In all but the kitchen and bathrooms, a flat, latex, water-base paint will be the best and easiest to work with.

When you buy enough to cover with two coats the area to be painted (no matter what it says about covering with only one coat on the label), get an additional quart of the same shade in the semigloss variety. This will be used for doors, windows, door frames and other trim surfaces that get a lot of handling. The semigloss can be wiped clean, whereas the flat variety (even though it's easier to work with and creates a warmer effect on a wall) cannot be scrubbed clean once the dirt is well rubbed in. Also pick up a can of premixed spackling paste and half a dozen sheets of medium sandpaper.

Room Preparation

The second step in the painting process is to prepare the room and the wall surfaces. Either remove all the furniture or stack it in a single pile covered with drop cloths. Next take down the curtains or fold them over the rods to get them out of the way. Then remove all hardware, picture and mirror hangers, switch plates, outlet plates and everything else attached to the wall that should not be painted or that will cause a skipped spot or drips.

If doors are to be painted, it may be easier to remove all door handles than to try to paint around them. The next step is to grab your can of spackle and a putty knife and inspect every square foot of wall area systematically for tack holes, nail holes, dents and doorknob or elbow holes. Simply press the spackle into the hole with the knife and then wipe it off as smoothly as possible. For larger holes patching plaster can be used (after gouging out the hole, leaving a lip around the edge to lock the patch in). If using spackling to fill a big hole, each layer of paste shouldn't be much more than 1/8" thick, because it will tend to shrink and crack if put on too thickly. So let each layer dry before building up the hole with another layer. If the hole is knocked all the way through the plaster or dry wall, then stuff in some wadded up newspaper to give the plaster filler a starting point. Never paint right over the freshly applied spackle, even though it says on the label that it's perfectly all right to do so. Let it sit for an hour or so; then it won't make a dull, discolored spot in the finished coat of paint.

Spackling may seem to be a tedious step, but if paint covers a multitude of sins, it's only spackling that makes this possible. With spackle, a paint job can make a room look brand-new; without it, the room simply looks a little cleaned up with all the same old flaws and holes showing through.

Once the spackling is on and dry, give the walls a light sanding to remove dirt that can discolor the new paint, and to smooth out the spackling job. Give the door and all gloss surfaces a little extra sanding to roughen the old paint so the new paint can get a good grip on the surface. Spread out the drop cloths and you're just about ready to start painting.

Painting

The first step after opening the paint can is to grab an ice pick or sharp punch and poke a few holes through the lip of the can (around the top where the lid of the can fits down into the lip). This will save all sorts of messes later on by allowing extra paint to drip back down into the can. If the job will require more than one gallon of paint to complete, pour both gallons (or more if necessary) into a large container and stir thoroughly. Then pour the mixed paint back into the cans. It is impossible to get two gallons to match absolutely exactly, and this mixing will remove the possibility of any "lines of demarkation" when switching from one gallon to the next one. This is especially important with darker shades of paint. Next give the paint a vigorous stirring again with the paddle or stick, lifting the thick paint off the bottom of the can to mix with the rest. If you wet the brush with water before dipping it into the paint for the first time, it will be easier to clean.

Painting in the corners of the walls and the ceiling is a good place to get under way. There are rollers which are made to fill in the line along these corners where the larger rollers can't quite reach, but they don't do as good a job as the traditional paintbrush. So save your money and spend a little extra time doing a good job in the corners with a two-inch trim brush. While you're at it, fill in around the window and door frames as well as any lights or hardware that the roller will have difficulty getting close to.

Next, using a piece of cardboard as a shield to protect the floor, paint around the bottoms of the walls and up over the bottom molding. Now, at last, you're ready to warm up the paint roller.

When you first pour an inch or so of paint into the roller pan, it usually won't need thinning. But if progress is slow or if the paint has a chance to stand in the pan for a while (or when you get down toward the bottom of the paint can), the paint may get a little thick, so just add a jigger or two of water. This will make the paint go a lot farther, not because of the added volume of the water but because of the added ease of spreading thinned paint.

113

The greatest aid to the painter at this stage of the game is an extension pole for the roller handle. This pole allows you to make much more uniform strokes no matter where you happen to be rolling. It also speeds up the job and permits you to watch the progress from a little distance; this helps you to spot irregularities while they're still wet.

Because the paint rollers are mounted in wire brackets from one end only (so you can pull them off for cleaning), the roller tends to push just a little harder on the end where the frame of the handle enters the roller mount. For this reason you'll tend to get heavier coverage along the line where this end runs down the wall. If you plan out your painting a little you can blend these heavier lines into a smooth, even coat. Work systematically across a wall or ceiling. If you start at the left end of a wall, for instance, roll down the wall with the handle bracket on the right so that the roller will fit into the corner. Then flip the roller handle over so that the supported end of the roller is to the left for the upward stroke position just to the right. The slightly heavier coverage on the left side of the roller will blend into the slightly heavier coverage of the last stroke. It's a minor point, but it tends to make good results easier to achieve.

The extension pole will save time as well as your back, but when using one, bear in mind that you will tend to roll faster with it. It's hard to notice while you're under way, but if the roller is turning too fast, tiny splatters will fly off the roller and slowly cover whatever carpeting or furniture might be below the stroke. So keep the strokes straight, systematic and not too fast.

When the corners are all painted in with the brush, and the wall areas are covered, you can step back and make sure that the roller strokes blend in fairly well with the corner brush strokes. The first coat sometimes won't look like much, especially if you're covering a dark color with a light one. But the second coat will go on much more easily and will require less time and paint. If the second coat goes on nicely but then allows show-through when it starts to dry, displaying the patches and roller marks of the first coat, don't be alarmed. When the paint is through drying, it will regain the smooth, uniform coverage it had when it first went on.

Semigloss paints, used for the window and door frames and such, are just a little harder to work with than flat latex paint. Whether you use oil-base enamels or semigloss water-base paint, both tend to run into drips somewhat easier on a vertical surface than do flat-finish paints; they require stricter attention to your brush and roller strokes.

Some semigloss paints don't seem to cover quite so well as others and may need three coats to do a good job on large areas where irregularities tend to show. They do better on trim and doors where a brush is used. Because the semigloss surface reflects a little and shows up brush stroke differences more than a flat paint, it's usually a good idea to go over a job just after the paint is on, giving it a smooth, regular brushing to make sure all the brush strokes are approximately parallel.

Entryways and porches can often double as a studio area and benefit visually in the bargain. This entry makes a well-lighted work place for ceramics and sewing.

This was once a U.S. Army temporary classroom. After the imaginative addition of used windows, well-thought-out (but inexpensive) wall treatments and interesting use of furnishings and curios, Sarge would hardly recognize the place.

When extra storage space is needed, but a framed-in closet box seems to be too much trouble, accordion doors can sometimes save the day. With a simple wooden framing around the edges, the doors themselves provide almost all the front of the closet enclosure.

Here a divider wall isolates a conversation area from the entryway while providing a natural border for the tile flooring.

Here both the divider wall and the closet frame the entryway and provide a natural opportunity to use tile flooring next to the door. The shutter doors can be fastened together in pairs with horizontal strips screwed to the back, making mounting easier and cheaper than double-jointed, bifold doors.

A den can be arranged to focus attention on the favorite piece in your memento collection. Here all eyes are directed toward the Oriental prayer rug.

When building a simple stained wood bar, decorative tiles can be inset into the surface to provide an attractive permanent hot plate.

Using contrasting wood textures can make the room more interesting and the job easier. Here rough timbers (rough-cut 1" x 6"s) complement the smoothness of the finished paneling while providing a divider between the sheets of paneling.

In rebuilding a room, one thing usually leads to another. In this case a strange urge to paint signal flags on the door led to a nautical theme that filled in many blank spots in the original design ideas. Flags spell out "E," "X," "I" and "T" (in case you're not up on your semaphore and can't find your way out).

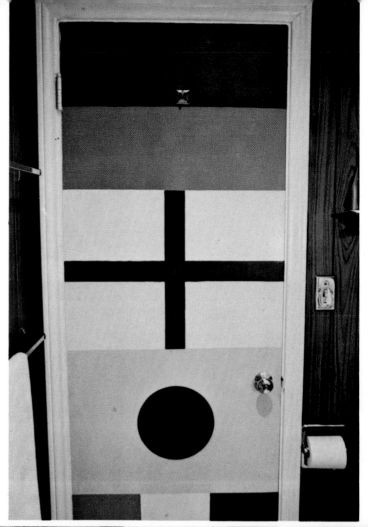

With the right kind of fencing and planting outside, it's occasionally possible to replace opaque glass with clear in a bathroom, bringing nature right in with you.

If you're building in new closet space, it's often an easy thing to include a dressing table area to one side. The countertop can be either table height (30") or dresser height (about 36"), depending on your preference. The mirror in this case is a cut-down veteran from a wrecking yard, framed with moldings to cover flaws around the edges.

The bed canopy is a simple and inexpensive way to add a lot of interest to a bedroom while providing an extra opportunity to carry out the pattern theme of the curtains.

To hide the entry into a kitchen, an L-shaped divider wall was framed up, covered with drywall and then plastered, using the technique discussed in the construction section. The texture is easier to apply and to patch than a flat surface.

The horizontal strips at the tops and bottoms of the cupboard doors are inset to join the boards, covering up their end grain at the same time.

When you can't quite find what excites you, perhaps a bold stroke will do the trick. When this builder was unable to find a table design that seemed worth the money, he discarded the whole idea of a conventional table and built a hanging version of his own that dominates the new look of the room (for a fraction of the cost of a new table).

When painting windows the challenge is to get a nice straight border along the edge of the frame where it meets the glass. A fierce controversy has raged between advocates of the various methods of getting a straight trim line. Some will tell you solemnly that the only way to bring it off is to use tape to mask the areas to be left free of paint; others maintain that using a paint shield, a good brush and a steady hand is the fastest way in the long run. A third group likes to slop it on good and thick, and then peel the paint off the glass with a razor blade after it has been allowed to dry for a day.

Painting trim lines by eye can be the fastest way to do it, but to do the job well *and* rapidly, you have to be highly practiced and in midseason form, or you can spend half an afternoon trying to get just one window done right.

We think the most dependable way to get the job done rapidly is to paint it on and then go back over the job with a razor scraper to take the excess paint off the glass. Of course, the less paint you get on the glass, the less you have to scrape off later, so try to hold your sloppings within reason. Scraping the paint off can be a simple process if you catch it just after it has begun to dry (so that it can be peeled off in strips). If allowed to dry hard as a rock, the paint will be much harder to scrape away, so try to catch up with your window scraping within a day or so of the original application.

Cleaning Up

If you're planning to continue with a second coat the next day, you can store the rollers and brushes in a bucket of water (or solvent if you're using oil-base paint) without doing too much damage. Try to place the brushes so that the bristles aren't splayed out in all directions. The best thing to do is give everything a thorough cleaning and drying after each day's work. But looking at things realistically, knowing that they'll be doing more the following day, most people won't do a really complete job of cleaning up after a long day of painting.

So you're better off letting everything soak overnight and then drying it out a little before use the next day. A brush or a roller will look clean and feel soft after a little rinsing under the faucet (or in the solvent). But unless *all* the paint is washed out of the inner bristles, they'll be hard as a rock the next day. When you can hold the brush upside down under a flowing faucet without a trace of paint pigment running down the sides, you can be fairly certain you won't find it stiff the next day.

Just a little stiffness can cause a lot of trouble in your application, so make sure your brushes and rollers are soft and manageable when you start up again, no matter what method you use.

Cheap, throwaway brushes are good only for just that: throwing away. They're a pain in the neck to work with, and they'll cost you a pretty penny in the long run (or they wouldn't be on the market in the first place). You'll find it cheaper and faster over a period of time to buy a couple of good quality brushes, get used to working with them and keep them in top condition.

A professional painter will spend an amazing amount of money on a good brush, and although you may not need a thirty-dollar model for your work, it's usually wise to avoid the very cheapest variety. There are also various chemical products on the market to save a brush if it gets left out by mistake. As these products work quite well, you can invest in a good brush and know that you can keep it awhile, even if by some strange accident you walk off and forget to wash it after the thrill of finishing up the job.

8

Installing Paneling

There is a fantastic variety of wood grains, textures, colors and even prints available in natural wood and masonite-backed paneling. Whether you're using a rough, textured masonite product or just the standard old prefinished wood paneling, the basic rules of installation are much the same.

Measuring

Once you've sorted through the folders available to you at most lumber and supply yards and have figured out which variety of paneling fits your needs and budget, the next step is to get an idea of how much material you'll need for the job. In measuring the room, either you can take a rough measurement and end up with a little left over; or if you're like some of us and want to get every ounce of value from every dollar spent, you can take the time to make a more careful measurement and usually save yourself the cost of one extra sheet of paneling per room.

To take a rough measurement, simply measure the total length of all the walls to be covered, divide the number of feet by four, and you'll have the number of sheets needed for the job. You'll notice, however, that a good bit of paneling will be taken up with window and door space and that there are times when a whole extra sheet will be bought just to fill in the narrow slice between a door and the corner of a room. So, to get the most from your panels, mark out on the walls themselves the areas to be covered by each sheet, bearing in mind what you'll have left over from window and door cuts to fill in an occasional small, odd-shaped area left uncovered by the panels.

Start your measurement in a corner of one of the blank walls to be covered, and work your way toward the window and door areas, measuring across four feet at a time (and sizing up the area covered as you go).

You will find that there are times when starting the paneling at the opposite end of a certain wall will alter the way the panels meet the window and door areas, so try all combinations of starting points on the walls in order to get the most from the panels. The object of the game is to leave the most usably shaped leftover scraps for possible use over the windows or between wall corners and door frames.

Preparing the Walls

Once you have made the plunge and bought your materials, the next step is to prepare the wall. The basic scheme is to get a smooth, flat, solid surface to attach the panels to, using either nails or a special paneling glue that comes in a caulking-tube gun. Most walls are straight and flat enough so that the paneling can be attached directly to the studs behind the existing surfacing. If, however, you find a wall that seems to wander all over the place and is a little too lumpy to provide a flat mounting surface, it might be a good idea to cover it with furring strips. These can be made from 1" x 2" construction grade fir, run along the wall horizontally in strips 16" apart on center (the distance between centers of the strips). Where the wall bends back away from the strips, place small shims or wedges of wood in the space between the wall and the back of the furring strip. Run 13"-long strips vertically, spaced 16" or 24" apart on center, so that they will cover behind the cracks of the butt joints between sheets of paneling. If the wall to be paneled is masonry, the furring strips can be attached with special masonry nails directly to the block.

In most cases all that has to be done to prepare the existing wall is to pull out all nails and picture hooks and rip off the existing trim moldings. The molding along the bottom of the wall doesn't present a problem—it comes off easily by prying with a long screwdriver driven down behind it with a hammer. If you happen to have carpeting in the room, the new paneling will usually look better with no bottom molding at all. And if you're dealing with wood floors, you may want to run a thin strip of inside corner molding along the bottom, according to taste.

The moldings that present a small problem are those that frame the doors, windows and closets. If these moldings are fairly substantial and a bit involved to replace, you may want to examine various ways to save them. You can cut the paneling very carefully to fit around them, possibly adding a very thin inside corner molding to cover the cut edge of the paneling along the edge of the door and window molding. Or you can peel off the molding very carefully by hammering in a chisel along the edge and prying it loose. Then the molding can be nailed back in place over the new sheet of paneling. Or you can discard the old molding altogether and replace it with new moldings that can be finished to match the new paneling. This is the best way to assure a totally new look for the room, especially around windows. You may hit on a combination of these that will suit the room and create the least trouble in construction. Window moldings can be replaced to create a fresh new look with little trouble, whereas closet moldings may be left in place to get around having to re-engineer the hanging of the doors. These moldings usually match the doors anyway, and form a better framing for them than a molding that matches the paneling. However, if the closet doors are to be replaced, then the easiest thing to do is rip out everything and begin anew.

Marking the Panels

If a panel is to be put up intact, then of course there's no marking or cutting to be done and you can skip to the next step of attaching the panels. But if there are window holes to be cut out, or electrical outlet box holes to be punched in the sheet, then the next step is to mark the sheet for cutting. Try to place it, face up, near the actual portion of wall to be covered so that you can refer to the wall to recheck whether your marking is correct. It seems a little silly to mention, but it's pretty easy to mark your cutout lines very carefully on the wrong surface of the paneling, or to do your measuring from the wrong edge, if you're not careful to refer back to the wall to double-check the shape of your panel cutout.

Measure up from the bottom and across from the side to locate the corner points of the window, door or outlet cutouts. Then use a framing square to mark the lines on the finished surface of the sheet. While marking, you may want to look over your choice of panels to see whether some will blend in better side-by-side than others. Keep this in mind when positioning the sheets.

When marking holes for electrical outlets and switches, mark enough area to allow only the outlets themselves (not the outlet cover plate) to stick through. This approximate hole shape can then be cut out with a hole saw attachment for the electrical drill (cutting out two 1-1/2" holes, one just over the other) or by drilling a starter hole and cutting out the shape with a keyhole saw.

Cutting

Because most paneling is usually pretty thin, it's sometimes difficult to get a nice straight cut if using an electrical hand saw. It sometimes helps to use the edge of a board to guide the edge of the saw along a straight cut. The board can be C-clamped to the sheet the needed distance from the cut line.

The deeper the blade of the saw is set, the straighter the cut tends to be; however, a deep-set blade will lift more splinters along the finished surface of the cut than a shallow-set blade. If you want the straightest, cleanest cut (where the cut cannot be covered by a molding for some reason), you can put down masking tape over the line, re-mark the line and make the cut with a cross-cut carpenter's hand saw. Have someone hold the sheet to keep the saw from binding; this helps keep the cut clean no matter what kind of saw is used.

In most cases, where the cuts will be covered with moldings, you'll probably end up using both the hand saw and the electric hand-held circular saw for best and speediest results. An electric saber saw must be held very firmly against the surface or it will become very hard to handle and to keep from marring the surface.

If a hole has to be cut for the center of a piece, drill a 1" starter hole somewhere in the area to be cut out. Then cut to the outline with a keyhole saw (or saber saw, keeping a steady pressure downward on the saw to prevent it from jumping around). After the cut has been started along the line, continue on with the hand saw or electric saw.

Mounting the Panels

After a panel has been cut, try it in place. Unless you're awfully good at marking and cutting, there will usually be a second cut necessary in the shape of the panel to make it fit. Once the panel fits over everything nicely, you can start to locate the studs, or vertical 2" x 4" framing, in the wall. In almost all cases, the studs behind the plaster or drywall are spaced so that there are 16" intervals between the centers of the studs; but since walls vary in length, you have to make sure, before starting to sink the nails, which end of the wall was used as a starting point for the spacing.

If you're certain the wall is to be covered with paneling shortly, then you can sink a few test holes with a hammer and nail until you find a stud. You can narrow down the choice, before punching holes in the wall, by tapping gently with a hammer on the wall. Where it sounds a little less hollow and drumlike than usual is the place to look for the stud. When you find one, try several other holes in the area to get and mark an exact positioning of the center of the stud. Measuring 16" from this point, you should encounter another, and so on. Make a mental note how far in the stud is positioned from the edge of the paneling.

On a great majority of panels are found longitudinal grooves marking the edges of the simulated paneling boards. These grooves appear to be in a somewhat random spacing in most types of paneling, but on every sheet there are two grooves that are spaced 16" apart in from the edge. Naturally, these grooves are more than handy for spacing your nails so that they'll hit the studs. If the first stud happens to fall 14" from the edge of the wall and consequently the edge of the sheet, then you know that you'll have to place the nails two inches to one side of the locating groove all the way down; the next row of nails will go two inches to the side of the following *locating* groove and so on.

If the last stud falls within four inches of the edge of the sheet, then the panel will be held firmly to the wall. But if more than four inches hangs out loose, then you may have to sink nails along the edge of the sheet, angled back into the plaster, to anchor the edge of the paneling to the wall.

Nails can be spaced every foot or so down the length of the studs. There are various extruded locking moldings for paneling that hold it in place a little more firmly than just nailing down the edges. These can also be used in corners to help create a finished look while you're mounting the paneling. But of course, these things all cost money, and although they add a little professional touch, you can get a nice uncluttered look if you do the job without them. Some varieties of masonite panels are manufactured with an interlocking edge that also makes a clean but strong mounting possible.

There are other ways, as well, to get away from a clumsy butt joint between panels. The style shown in the illustrations places a rough-hewn timber vertically between sheets to form a natural border for the panels. This can be re-created on a wall with rough-cut 1" x 6"s to give the same effect. Nailing on vertical, floor-to-ceiling battens every 16" to 24" can also add interest to paneling and cover butt joints at the same time.

A good size nail to use for all-around panel installation is a 1-1/2" or 1-3/4" finishing nail. After all the sheets are in place with the moldings attached, you can go over every sheet with a hammer and nail set or center punch, and give each nail an extra tap or two with the hammer and punch—just enough to set the nail head down into the panel wood but not enough to knock it through. Then go over the sheets and moldings once more with a putty stick to fill in over the nail heads. These sticks, which look like overgrown crayons, can be found in racks at the paint department in a shade to match every wood grain. Get a shade that's just a little darker than the total color effect of the panel (since the wood grain has a variety of shades in most cases). To apply, simply draw over the hole with the point until the hole is filled, then wipe the surface area clean with a rag.

Moldings

A handy tool to have when putting on the corner moldings is a miter box of some kind to get uniform cuts. When marking the corner molding, mark the longest dimension of the molding (since the piece will usually be cut on an angle), and then draw a rough line showing the direction that the cut is to be angled. The most difficult part of cutting molding isn't getting the over-all dimension right, but rather getting the *direction* of the cut correct. Many's the time we've cut a piece to just the right length, only to find that it should have been angled down a different side.

In corners where you have three pieces of molding all coming together at the same point (usually two horizontal and one vertical) take the time to figure the simplest way for them to meet according to their cross-sectional shapes before cutting the first one. In almost every case it's worthwhile to paint, varnish or stain the moldings to match the panel sheets *before* nailing them in place. This may seem pretty tedious, especially as the moldings come at the end of the project when you're anxious to get everything wrapped up as quickly as possible. But moldings are very difficult to stain in place without getting the stain all over the adjoining paint or panel, even if masking tape is used. A piece of molding can be stained and wiped in a matter of seconds before it's nailed up, but it can easily take the better part of half an hour to get edged properly once it's in place.

In a small room, such as a bathroom, you may want to try to get away from the use of moldings altogether, since they can add greatly to the "heaviness" of the look of a wall. There are a few simple tricks that can be used to reduce the number of moldings normally required to cover exposed edges of cuts.

If a ceiling covering, such as some type of acoustical tile, is to be used, put this in after the paneling is in place. The uniform edges of the tiles will butt up smoothly against the panels and cover the exposed top edge of the wall

121

covering. Along the bottom edge of the panels, as we've said earlier, a thick shag carpet will cover any irregularities where the floor meets the bottom of the paneling.

To get around having to use corner moldings, space the first panel to be installed about 1/4" away from the edge of the wall, allowing a 1/4" strip of uncovered wall to show along the side in the corner. Panel the rest of this wall in the usual fashion, making certain that the last cut-off edge fits snugly against the face of the next adjoining wall. Start paneling the next wall by butting the smooth, ready-made edging of the paneling up against the face of the last sheet of paneling on the previous wall covered—concealing the exposed cut-off edge in the corner. Continue around the walls of the room, covering the last cut-off sheet on the previous wall with the uncut panel in each corner until reaching the corner where you began. Then the cut-off edge of the last sheet of paneling of the last wall can be inserted in the 1/4" wide strip left uncovered in the beginning; in this way all the cut-off edges will be hidden from view without the need for cumbersome moldings.

When replacing an old door or window molding (or any molding, for that matter), inspect the racks of molding at the lumberyard to choose the one you like, no matter what it was originally made for. There are only a few basic categories of moldings despite all the sizes and styles that meet the eye: outside corner molding, inside corner molding and butt-joint cover moldings. You may well find a completely different size and style that fills your needs better than the original of the recommended type of molding. Mahogany moldings seem to take stains that approximate the tone of the darker wood grains better than do pine moldings.

Replacing Outlet and Switch Covers

After all the sheets of paneling are in place, the last step is to replace the hardware on the new surface. In most cases flush-mounted towel racks and the like can be reattached to the new wall. In the case of electrical switches and outlets, however, a few modifications will have to be made first.

Because the switch plate covers will be attached 1/4" or 3/16" farther out than their original positions, it's necessary to move the switches and outlets out the same distance to meet them.

Switches and outlets are held in place by two small bolts, one at the top and one at the bottom of the units. To space them out to the new position, you can do either of two things: If the hole cut in the paneling is close enough to the position of the bolts, they can be unscrewed, the unit pulled out from behind the paneling, and the bolts replaced tightly, holding the flat mounting brackets of the unit onto the new wall surface. Then the switch or outlet cover plate can be replaced.

However, if the hole for the unit is too large to allow the mounting bracket to sit down firmly on the new surface, then the bolts can be removed and washers or slightly oversized nuts placed between the original mounting and the back of the bracket, with the bolts running through the spacers.

Before *any* work is done to reposition the switch or outlet units, MAKE ABSOLUTELY SURE THE POWER TO THESE UNITS HAS BEEN TURNED OFF.

9

Plaster Textures

When we were looking around for interesting stucco-like textures to provide a contrasting wall covering to complement the tone of wood paneling, we found almost as many different methods of getting a good, rough "authentic" Spanish look as there were people to ask. Everyone seemed to have his own version of the real secret of creating the look of a Spanish wall with modern materials—and all were duly tried. But they all seemed to give the same sort of effect: the kind seen on Spanish style taco and hot-dog stands (that have been textured by a plasterer who has spent his whole life perfecting a textureless wall and now is asked to put a texture on one).

Special trowel techniques were tried, textured paints were rolled with textured rollers, and mops were dipped into the compound used for smearing over the joints between sheets of wallboard; still nothing came out that looked remotely like a Spanish wall.

Finally in desperation someone asked how the unschooled peasants did it in the old days—and the answer was found: They used their hands. To get a Spanish wall texture simply put the plaster on with your hands and try to make it as smooth as you can. Presto! There's your texture. Admittedly, not everyone will choose this style, but if you're looking for much the same plaster effect as in the illustrations, here's how to go about it.

Applying the Plaster

First, cover the floor area with drop cloths. Then nail chicken wire to the studs in the wall with roofing nails or staples, covering the entire wall with the wiring (although the plaster can be applied directly to the new gypsum board drywall and it will hold reasonably well). Apply the plaster along the top of the wall first, working down toward the bottom. With a bucket of water and a large sponge soak the first part of the wall to be covered—an area about six feet wide by three feet high.

Actually, the material used to cover the wall isn't plaster, strictly speaking, but rather a premixed concoction available at most lumber and supply yards called "plaster mix," which is used for such surfaces. It's gray, instead of

124

white like plaster, and is far easier and more economical to work with. While plaster of Paris or patching plaster has a way of setting up hard as a rock just about the time you get your tools all set, plaster mix is very well mannered and will stay workable for about twenty minutes—just about the time needed to apply all you can mix in one batch. It's not our place to advertise products, but there are times when only one product will create the effect desired. In this case Sacrete Plaster Mix is the brand to look for in order to get this particular texture. None other seems to do the job.

Mix a bucketful with water so that it's not too runny to stand by itself, yet wet and smooth enough to be squeezed through your fingers. Then, starting at the top and working across, begin spreading the stuff on to about a 3/4" average thickness with your hands. Some will fall onto the drop cloths and can be scooped up and thrown back into the bucket to be mixed in with the rest. Smooth out the surface to get rid of fingermarks that are too noticeable. When the surface is reasonably flat, pat it with a palmful of slightly wetter mix from the bucket to create a raised "stipple" effect.

Try to mix in all the leftover plaster in the bottom of the bucket with each new batch. Work your way across and down the wall, wetting each area before covering it. When the wall is covered, stand back and view the effect and then make any changes in the texturing patterns that have developed naturally. While the mix is still fairly wet you may want to trim up any edges next to the woodwork or paneling with a kitchen knife. If a particular area seems to lack a certain appeal, you can always go back over it as many times as you please to rework and add more mix. Plaster mix is a very forgiving medium to work with and can be carved very easily. Like any plaster wall, it's vulnerable to kicks and blows. But a rough-textured wall is far easier to patch because the break at the patch line can be hidden in the texture itself.

Patching Plaster

When a plaster wall succumbs to the ravages of water or has a hole punched in it by a misdirected foot, the first step toward patching the wound is to get rid of all the loose material and to establish a strong overhanging lip around the hole which will help hold the patch in place.

In a bathroom, where water has done dirty work to a smooth plaster wall, you may suddenly find with a sinking feeling that what appeared to be a simple, small blemish on the otherwise smooth surface is actually a substantial growth of powderlike substance which has eaten away the plaster underneath the paint all the way down to the floor. When this is the case, especially in the bathroom where the condition will almost certainly repeat itself sooner or later, the time may be ripe to think about an alternative wall covering that will stand up to the room's conditions a little better.

But if you decide to stick with the plaster concept for another season at least, the only thing to do is grit your teeth and chip away every last inch of corroded plaster, no matter how well hidden it may be beneath the protective coating of paint. When the only plaster left on the wall is good and sound, carve away the exposed edge of the good plaster, leaving a little lip around the area that has been eaten away.

The greatest problem in applying a patch to a plaster wall lies in the fact that the surrounding wall usually leeches the water out of the new plaster, making it set up before you have time to get it smoothed out—and sometimes before you have time to get it smeared on. To hold this to a minimum, thoroughly wet the surrounding area, and the part that's been eaten away, with a sponge and then apply the patching plaster in a fairly wet mixture, smoothing it out immediately with a trowel. The best idea is to mix small amounts and fill up a patch with repeated applications, eventually building up a smooth surface.

Drywall

Plastering a whole wall in the usual, professional way is a little beyond the scope of the beginning amateur builder. However, you may run across a situation in which the installation of drywall-gypsum board is the most obvious answer to providing a paintable new wall surface.

Drywall board comes in 4' x 8' sheets and can be either scored with a knife and then broken along a line, or simply cut to shape with a hand saw. The sheets are nailed in with 1-5/8" or 1-7/8" coated drywall nails driven into the wall studs, as with paneling.

If you look at the side edges of drywall board, you'll see that the thickness of the board starts to pinch in, tapering slightly toward the edge. This tapering allows a joining tape to be laid over the crack between two sheets and then a filler compound to be smoothed on to make a perfectly flat joining of the two sheets.

You'll need a special drywall joint compound, a roll of wallboard tape, a 4"-wide joint finishing knife and a 10"-long joint finishing knife to do the job.

Three applications of the compound are usually needed to make a good joint. Spread the first layer along the area next to the joint on both sides, laying a strip down the joint about 3" wide. Then lay the tape onto this layer, directly over the joint, and smooth the tape into the compound with the knife. When the first coat is dry, lay on a thin coat to smooth out the joint a little farther to both sides. Use the longer knife to apply the last thin coat, feathering the edges of the joint smoothly to both sides. When the joints have dried for a day or so, sand the surface smooth with medium grade sandpaper wrapped around a flat board. Clean the sanding dust from the wall, and you're ready to paint.

Whenever an inside or outside corner is encountered much the same process goes on. At inside corners, the tape is laid into the corner, and then the joint is smoothed out with compound, feathering the edges to both sides. When an outside corner is rounded, a special metal beading is nailed on first and then layers of compound are laid over this, smoothing it back into the surface of the wall. Of course, all nailheads are smoothed over with compound, using the 4" joint finishing knife.

126

10

Wallpaper

As we've said before, wallpapering is no longer the test of a man that it once was. Generally you'll find that there are two categories of wallpaper: the regular, standard pulp papers and the thicker, vinyl-coated variety, suitable for bathrooms and kitchens and sometimes children's rooms. Both types can be found in regular and prepasted form, and the regular is just about as easy to put on as the prepasted. Although the latter style is a bit handier, there isn't enough difference to warrant abandoning a favorite pattern just because it isn't prepasted.

Buying the Paper

This is the hardest step to understand in the whole process of wallpapering. Choosing which pattern will do the job is no special trick, but figuring out how much you'll need can get confusing at times.

If the room tends to have a lot of water vapor in the air a good deal of the time, or if there's a chance that the walls will be subjected to rubbed-in dirt, then stick to the vinyl-coated, waterproof, washable papers when looking over the choices. There are literally thousands of papers and patterns to pick from, and the more you can narrow down what you're looking for, the less time it will take you to pore over the sample books. Most of them specialize in one sort of paper or another, so you can generally flip through all the books in a store hurriedly to find which books seem to have the kind of paper you're after. Then you can sit down and spend a more leisurely hour or so thumbing over the choices in the category you need.

It's hard at times to guess what a page full of paper will look like when it covers a whole wall. The only hint we've found is that papers with dark backgrounds are a good deal more overwhelming when viewed on a whole wall than when seen in the book. If a certain paper seems to be close to the mark, but you're still not certain, make every effort to borrow the book over a weekend so you can prop up the page in place and try various design tests on it (see the General Ideas section).

Wallpaper rolls come in various widths from about 18" to 22", and the only standard of measurement is that each roll must contain at least thirty-six square feet of paper. The most popular width seems to be about 20" or 20-1/2", which means that you can plan on getting about twenty-one running feet of paper in a roll. For some strange reason wallpaper is almost always sold in double rolls, which means you have to buy two rolls at a time or pay extra for a single roll.

As in paneling there are two ways to figure the material you'll need: the easy way that will give some leftover, or the more involved way that can often save you the price of an extra roll per room.

You can multiply the length of the walls to be covered by the height (usually eight feet) and then subtract the square footage taken up by windows and doors. Divide this total by 36 to find the number of rolls needed to cover the area. Add an extra roll per average room for the trim wastage.

If you want a closer estimate of how much you'll need to do the job, mark the actual walls to be covered at intervals equal to the width of the paper, and then measure vertically the amount of running feet needed to cover the wall. Sometimes, by changing the starting point for your width measurement, you can end up with a more efficient use of the paper. For instance, when laid out one way, there may be a lot of paper trimmed away for a door. To avoid this wastage, it may be possible to place the starting point of the paper so that it will border the side of the door. Then a short piece can be used to cover the area over the door; about five running feet of paper can be saved in the process. Try to avoid layouts that lead to long trim cuts that waste a lot of paper.

Bear in mind when laying out the job that there are basically two types of patterns: those which do not interlock visually with adjoining strips of paper on the wall, and those that do. An interlocking (or matching) pattern usually has the pattern running right off the edge of the paper, to be continued on the adjacent strip, whereas a noninterlocking pattern can usually be recognized by plain background color that continues out beyond the pattern to the edge of the strip. Vertical stripes are also a noninterlocking pattern. The reason we belabor this point is that when using an interlocking pattern you'll need more paper to cover the same wall area.

In most cases you will have to cut a strip of interlocking pattern paper extra long so that you can line up the pattern with the previous strip to get the patterns exactly matched and aligned. With a noninterlocking pattern, of course, this step isn't necessary and you can cut off the piece much closer to the actual length needed for coverage.

You can count on getting about thirty-six *running* feet of coverage from a *double* roll of interlocking paper and about thirty-eight or thirty-nine *running* feet of coverage from a *double* roll of noninterlocking pattern paper.

Wall Preparation

The walls are prepared in almost the same way as they would be for a painting job. All nails and obstructions should be removed. All holes bigger than a nail hole should be filled with spackling paste. All lumps should be scraped away; and a light sanding job just to get rid of surface dirt wouldn't hurt in most cases. Actually, sanding is usually necessary on gloss paint surfaces in order to provide a good grip for the paste.

On the day before you plan to start papering, mix up a small batch of paste (an inexpensive vegetable paste available at the lumber and supply yard or wallpaper store), and paint the wall area with the paste, making certain that no lumps of paste are left on the surface. Although the claim is made for some papers that they don't require this step, which is called "sizing," it's a simple fifteen-minute job that will make laying up the paper just a bit easier the next day.

Even though there's nothing magic about putting up wallpaper, we've found that the best condition for working with it is absolute solitude. There are no special skills involved, but you have to keep your mind on your work, and the less audience you have, the less trouble you generally have.

You'll need a wide paintbrush, a gallon bucket, a sponge, some drop cloths, a razor knife with a good supply of blades, a framing square or T-square, a yardstick and two 2' to 4' sticks. With the prepasted variety, you'll also need a soaking pan, usually available at the same place you bought the paper.

Since pasting is such an easy step, many people go ahead and paint on paste right over the prepasted surface of such papers—just to be sure (and to save the cost of the soaking pan). To combat this conservation, there are often witty little notes to be found on the rolls of prepasted paper telling such customers that they really don't have to bother with the paste anymore, and to have faith in the prepasted paper when properly soaked in the water pan.

If you still want to hang back and apply paste to prepasted papers, it should at least be diluted by using about twice the amount of water recommended on the package.

Prepasted paper is placed in the water-filled soaking pan and the whole affair is then positioned at the bottom of the wall area to be covered. The wall is painted with water, to prevent leeching, and then the paper is drawn out, smoothed on the wall and cut off.

With the more traditional papers, one method of application that we've found to be absolutely dependable runs something like this:

Mix the paste as directed on the package and let it sit for about half an hour. Then spread out a drop cloth on the floor of the room to a length of about ten feet. Place the roll of paper on the cloth so that it will unroll backside-up, place a stick across the end of the paper to keep it from rerolling and then unroll the paper to about nine or ten feet, placing the other stick under the roll to prevent it from rolling back.

When the paste is ready, paint the wall with a light, lump-free coat, then cut the first length of paper about 4" longer than the height of the wall (using the square and razor knife); paint the length of wallpaper with paste, making certain no spots have been missed.

Check the pattern to be sure which end of the cut piece is the top, and then fold the bottom end back to about the middle of the piece so that the pasted side is folded back onto itself. Fold the top end back on itself in the same way, grab the edges of the paper where it loops back over on the top end, and carry the paper to the wall area to be covered.

Double check to make certain that the pattern is right side up, and then grab the top corners of the paper and let it unfold, while placing the piece into position with the top edge overlapping the top of the wall about an inch.

Line up the side edges of the paper, and smooth it on the wall firmly. Then let the bottom half of the paper unfold downward, align the side edges and smooth it down.

Next smooth out the paper with your hands (some people use a rubber squeegee), starting at the top of one side edge, moving across and down the paper systematically, pushing all air bubbles out to the side. Then go over the whole surface with a slightly damp sponge in the same way to remove both glue on the surface and any remaining air pockets under the paper. It's sometimes necessary to sight across the paper so you can see the light reflected off the surface in order to spot the last few air bubbles. When you can run the sponge over the surface without a telltale crackling sound, the bubbles are gone.

Trim away the overhang at the top and bottom and you're ready to start on the next strip. (If you're working with an interlocking pattern, cut the following pieces from the roll nine to twelve inches longer than the height of the wall so that the pattern can be aligned with the first strip.)

Leave all trimming around edges and frames until the strip is in place, and then force the paper well down into the corner of the edging and trim with the razor knife. A roller knife, which looks like a pizza cutter, can help make the corner cuts. A dull blade in the razor knife can cause tears in the wet paper, so keep a sharp edge in the knife. There are razor knives available with breakaway blades that provide a new edge quickly and inexpensively every time you snap away part of the blade. If there is a frame to be trimmed around both horizontally and vertically, cut a slice away from the corner point.

Sometimes a strip of paper will get off on the wrong foot and you'll find that you can't quite get it in position without crinkling it. When this happens, peel off a good portion of the strip, leaving just enough in place to keep the strip from falling off the wall. The loosened portion can then be repositioned in the correct spot and smoothed flat; the portion that wasn't peeled away can then be pulled back and repositioned—all without having the paper come loose from the wall and fall all over you.

As the day wears on, try to keep the paste well mixed, and add a bit of water from time to time as it begins to thicken. If you're working in a bathroom or kitchen, it's best to remove every possible piece of hardware from the wall prior to papering, including even mirror cabinets and anything that can be unscrewed or unbolted from the wall. It's almost always faster to remove an obstruction rather than to try to get a good trim line around it—and the resulting finish is far more professional-looking.

If you have an adjoining wall that is not going to be papered, but which could use some of the same flavor, you can cut out a few figures from the wallpaper pattern (provided the pattern has separate figures), and then paste these as artfully as you can on the unpapered wall. It's a simple way to use up scraps to convey the papered effect on an additional wall without added expense; it is also a good way to cover flaws in the unpapered wall.

Save the larger scraps from the project for repairs and reference when matching the paper at a later date if need be. Large scraps can also be used to line drawers and cover shelves for a nice finished look to the room.

11

Special Interest Wall Textures

The methods used in attaching the various imitation and special interest textures vary a great deal from product to product and there is usually ample instruction included with the material when you buy it. Rather than try to list every method for every product, we'll just stick to a few general rules that we've found to be helpful whenever installing these special interest textures.

Adhesives

Many stick-on products are held to the wall surface with a thick, brown tarry adhesive with a particularly pungent odor. This glue has proved itself to be worthy stuff, holding the most unlikely combinations of materials together with a good, lasting bond. You can help it work a little better by roughing up the wall with sandpaper to get rid of any unseen dirt or grease. Whenever a canned product smells strongly (such as this adhesive), check the label for warnings about flammability. If the makers suggest keeping it away from an open flame in a closed area, it's a good idea to shut off the pilot lights. There are items in the newspapers every day showing that they're not kidding when they say the stuff will burn if it gets a chance. Once the drying agent has done its job and the smell tapers off a little, of course, there's no more danger.

Shingles

Shingles create an interesting effect inside a room. But for some reason, although most people start off all right, nailing on the bottom row first and then overlapping each succeeding row, working up the wall, they forget the important final step. When the last row is in place at the top of the wall, be sure to nail on an added row of shortened, cut-off shingles to maintain a uniform thickness over the entire area all the way to the top edge.

Weathered Lumber

Naturally weathered lumber can also give interest to a room. A further modification on this theme which seems to work out well is to sand the boards with medium or fine sandpaper, just enough to bring out the highlights of the grain but not enough to remove the texture. Weathered boards can also be

Corkboard, backed by plywood, can be built in as an attractive, integral part of the shelving in a workroom, providing an unobtrusive bulletin board that can blend into the background if the room is to be cleaned up and used for other purposes from time to time.

133

used as raised panels mounted on a smooth, contrasting texture as a background. Of course, it's nearly impossible to find enough good, long pieces of weathered lumber to cover a wall from floor to ceiling. The use of shorter boards, placed end to end, seems to create an attractive wall, even though the same practice with new lumber would not get the same effect.

Bricks

When applying any form of "individually laid" imitation bricks, try to watch the pattern of dark and light colors you create as the bricks go on, so that you don't end up with all the dark bricks in one patch. When attaching these bricks, start at the top row and work down so you'll be absolutely certain that the top row fits well along the ceiling corner joint. It's somehow more natural to have a molding along the foot of the wall, if one is needed to cover a row of bricks that had to be trimmed to fit.

With glued-on bricks, spread about an 18" x 30" area with glue using a serrated trowel (which keeps the amount of glue uniform). Then start laying the bricks, but don't continue on up to the very edge of the glue patch. Leave a wide border at the edges of the glued area so that the next area can be covered without getting the stuff all over the bricks that were just laid.

Corkboard

Textured fabric over corkboard makes an attractive place for your favorite graphics without looking like an out-of-place bulletin board. The cork can be nailed to plywood, then fabric can be attached with spray-on glue, giving two coats to both surfaces before smoothing the fabric onto the cork. A variety of different metal and wood frame moldings can then be attached with screws, nails or linoleum glue. Uncovered corkboard can give an interesting effect too; however, it's not very durable.

12

Carpeting

Before committing yourself to a carpet of any size, it's often educational to examine the back of the type you are considering for clues to how the material will wear in years to come. A good carpeting will have a double layer of backing bonded together. If there are many pinholes of light coming through from behind the carpeting when creased, you might check the price again to make sure you're not paying a premium for it. Spread the loops apart to see how thickly they're spaced. If there aren't enough loops per square inch, the carpet may well start to look bald before long.

Of course, there are times when you have to take what you can get, and sometimes it may actually be better for the house to have inexpensive carpeting over a larger area than would be possible with a really fine carpet. Make certain that what you get is at least up to the standards expected within its price range.

For use in small, high-traffic areas like bathrooms and kitchens, you may want to hold out for an end piece from a roll of really good material. End pieces and remnants can be found at bargain prices if you keep your eye on the stock of the larger carpet suppliers. A good nylon is what is called for in bathrooms to withstand both the moisture and the wear.

How Carpet Is Laid

The more approved way to put down carpet, especially for large areas, is to use tack strips around the edges. These are slats about the thickness of a yardstick with fastening nails sticking down through at regular intervals, and hundreds of little nail points sticking up at an angle through the top surface. These strips are nailed to the floor 3/8" out from the walls, with the gripping points sticking up and angled toward the adjacent wall.

The rubber carpet pad is laid down and trimmed with a razor knife to fit just inside these tack strips. Then the carpeting is laid over the pad and strips, and positioned to get the most out of the cut of the carpet within the shape of the room so that the seams will be at a minimum.

Next, any seams are sewn from the back and the carpeting is pushed down onto the tack strips along one side. The carpet is smoothed out and then with the use of stretching tools (which grip the carpet, allowing you to stretch it tight away from the fastened side) is pulled tight and pushed down into the gripping teeth of the opposite tack strip. The teeth of the tack strip, because they angle away from the opposite strip and toward the wall, will hold the backing of the carpet firmly in tension. Then the edging of the carpet can be trimmed by pushing it as far as possible down into the corner and cutting it with a razor knife. If the carpeting is to be laid over concrete, special masonry nails may be needed to hold down the tack strips.

Cutting the Carpet for Bathrooms and Kitchens

When cutting a carpet to shape for a bathroom or kitchen, the job is made a little tougher by the intricate outline that must be followed around the cabinets and fixtures. If there is already a carpet in the room, then the task can be a little simpler. Place the new carpet upside down on a flat surface. Make a note of where the old carpet shape could be improved to fit the outline of the room better. Then place the older carpet over the new—also upside down. Draw around the outline of the old carpet onto the backing of the new one with a felt tip pen (allowing for the improvements) and then cut along this line with the razor knife.

The most difficult place to fit a carpet in a bathroom (if you don't have a pattern) is usually the outline around the toilet. One way to cut this outline is to place the uncut carpeting roughly in position in the room, draped over the seat of the toilet. Then push the carpeting down so that it is approximately flat in front of the base; mark a 3" diameter rough circle about 1-1/2" up from the border of the base in front. Next cut a straight line back from the center of this circle directly to the back of the toilet; continue to cut all the way off the edge of the carpet piece. Cut out the rough circle, and then cut the rest of the carpeting to shape. Once the carpeting is in place in the room, the portion surrounding the circle and straight cut can be draped around the base of the toilet and pushed down into the corner of the toilet base and floor on each side in turn; then the outline of the toilet base can be cut to exact shape.

Padding

If you're planning to include a pad under the new carpeting, cut the pad to shape by placing it in position (usually with the longest straight edge along the longest straight wall), then cut away the excess down to about three or four inches oversize around the remaining sides. Next tack the pad in place along the edge used as the starting point (so that the pad won't be pulled away from its position while cutting the other sides), then firmly force the padding down into the corners along the edges and cut with a razor knife.

When the pad is cut to shape, note down the improvements that could be made in its shape, and then place the pad upside down over the back of the carpeting. Mark the shape, make the improvements and cut along the outline on the back of the carpet. Be certain that the pad lies with the bottom side up on the back of the carpet. Old carpeting makes great padding. It can be left in place under the new to give a soft, luxurious feel, saving lots of work in the bargain.

Fastening the Edge of the Carpet

If the new carpet is to be cut off at the threshold of a room, with the old carpet continuing on into the next room, then the question of what to do with the edging of the new carpet arises at this point.

Carpet tacks tend to make an uneven edge when used to hold the threshold border of a new carpet over an old. There are a number of covers available at most supply yards in both metal and wood. These work admirably, but they can look a little bulky and usually require the door to be shortened.

A third alternative is to glue the edge of the new carpet to the old, to prevent it from curling up under use. The best adhesive we've found for this purpose is the flexible type used to bond soles to shoes. The adhesive is applied hot with a special electric "glue gun." Once a beading is squeezed out along the area just under the new edging, the carpet can be held down onto the hot glue and the whole thing will set up in a matter of seconds.

This glue holds onto any porous or fibrous surface like grim death, and the speed with which it sets up makes the gun a very satisfying tool to work with. Just about the time you begin to tire of holding the two pieces together, the glue is set, and you're ready to move on to the next step. Although the tool was originally developed for industrial needs only, its wide applications to practically any kind of household adhesive job has spread its fame until the gun and glue kits are available at most lumber and supply yards for under ten dollars.

As we said earlier, it may be a good idea to leave the carpeting unfastened to the floor in bathrooms, except under the sill at the door. This makes cleaning and drying easier. As the carpet shape is usually small, with an irregular outline, it will generally lie flat with no help from fasteners anyway.

13

Cork, Linoleum and Ceramic Tile Floors

If you prefer to have a hard surface flooring, the preparation of the old floor is a little more involved. With cork or linoleum tiles, a sound, flat surface is a must in order to give the tiles a firm grip.

Preparing the Floors

For old floors in reasonably good condition (or new cement slab floors previously uncovered), simply sand off the dirt and old wax with coarse sandpaper, giving the adhesive a solid grab on the old flooring.

If only a few small holes are found, you may want to simply fill the depressions with a mixture of plastic cement, smoothed off at the top with a trowel, to create a firm, flat surface for the new floor covering.

Since the great majority of bathrooms which are ripe for a rebuilding job make use of some form of linoleum floor covering, you may want to determine just why it didn't work out in the first place, before you commit yourself to re-creating the same conditions.

When the question of a proper flooring for these new-fangled indoor bathrooms first came up, linoleum (having a surface that is impervious to water) was the obvious answer. But the fact remains that, although water can't flow through linoleum, it doesn't hesitate to flow around it (especially next to the tub) and down into the woodwork. Of course, water also flows there when a carpet is used; but whereas a carpet will allow the wood to dry out between drenchings, the waterproof surface of the linoleum serves to keep the wood underneath from drying out thoroughly. The result is usually a rotted floor.

Repairing a Rotted Wood Floor

One of the first steps for recovering a floor with new tiles is to somehow patch together the rotted wood under the old covering. If the previous flooring was of the sheet linoleum variety, instead of tile, you may find that the sheet extends up the wall several inches. Since this visual effect isn't usually the most attractive, you may want to remove the side wall edgings of the old floor before putting on the new tiles.

138

With a hammer and an old screwdriver, pry the metal stripping of the linoleum away from the wall and then pull back the edges until the flap tears free from the linoleum glued to the floor. This flap will generally tear off in a gradually tapered rip. But if it breaks off at a certain point, leaving a sudden drop in the floor surface, chisel this lip away until there is a fairly smooth transition from the bare flooring in the corner to the old linoleum surface over the rest of the floor.

If a small part of the wood flooring is rotted, it may be possible to cut away the area carefully with an electric handsaw and then fill the hole with a plywood patch of the same thickness as the original flooring.

If the flooring is pretty well gone in several spots, it may be easier and more satisfactory in the long run to cover the entire floor with a layer of 3/4" or 1" thick exterior plywood, nailed down directly to the old flooring joists. This will provide a good, solid, flat surface to make laying a new floor easy. To make a floor pattern, tape sheets of cardboard or paper together; cut out a pattern that fits down on the floor; then use the pattern to mark the exact outline of the floor directly onto the plywood before cutting. If the plywood has only one finished side, make certain the pattern lies on the top surface of the plywood right side up.

If two sheets of plywood must be used to cover the floor area, nail the butted edges down firmly so that the surfaces are aligned and there is no squeak when you step on the joint.

Once the floor is ready, you can begin the process of laying the tiles. Again, we don't recommend the use of sheet linoleum for floor areas because the techniques involved are beyond the scope of most amateur builders.

Laying the Tiles

Linoleum or cork tiles are laid with a thick, brown, tarry adhesive, applied with a serrated trowel which helps maintain a uniform thickness. The size and shape of the serrating determine how much glue is spread on; so ask the advice of someone at the lumberyard to get the right serration for the particular glue used on the job. Often the label on the can will describe the type of spreader to be used.

Make certain all gas jets are off in the room to be worked in. Spread the adhesive along the longest straight edge of the floor with the trowel, forcing the teeth down onto the old floor surface. Spread the glue on a large enough area so that a row of tiles can be laid; then more glue can be spread without getting glue on the tiles just put down. Lay the tiles systematically, making certain that each tile is pressed close to adjacent tiles. Most edge tiles can be cut with a straight edge and a linoleum knife; the more stubborn materials may have to be cut with metal shears or with an old blade on the table saw.

At each door frame the tile edging should be covered with a threshold plate. Usually the old one can be reused by taking it off, laying the tile up under its position, and then replacing it (using longer screws if need be). The new floor can usually be walked on after a few hours, but check the label to make sure.

139

Ceramic Tile Floors

If your existing carpeting is not so fresh as it once was, you may want to explore the idea of cutting away worn areas in the entryway and dining room and replacing the carpet with Spanish or Mediterranean type ceramic tile, which can create a very authentic effect (with a little softer surface). If the under flooring is concrete, however, you may want to use thin-set ceramic floor tiles, which are available in a great variety of shapes and colors. The best selection and prices can usually be found at a tile supplier rather than at a lumber and supply yard, which normally stocks only the fastest-moving products. Authentic floor tiles are easy to lay and will last the life of the house even in the areas of extremely high wear and tear.

Once the area to be tiled has been uncovered down to the slab (and the surrounding carpeting has been covered with polyethylene to protect it from spills) the project can get under way, starting with a good scrubbing of the concrete slab. Then the tile should be laid in place, without cement, to test different positionings and to mark any edge tiles that may have to be cut. One good way to make exact cuts is to use a masonry blade in the electric circular saw. Clamp the tile piece to a board with C-clamps mounted on both sides of the cut, and then run the blade along the cut line, making just a shallow scoring line. Repeat this, traveling over the same line several times, cutting a little deeper with each pass until you think it's safe to try breaking the tile along the line. If you want to be extra safe, you can keep cutting over the same line until the tile is cut all the way through. Some sort of glasses or protective goggles should be worn whenever cutting masonry with a carborundum blade.

You can also cut tile with one of the new, round diamond dust blades that fit into hacksaws. These do a good job on almost any hard material and aren't so expensive as they sound.

Once all the tiles are laid and you have checked which ones need cutting, they can be removed and placed to one side, keeping them in order.

When you're all set to go, soak the area of the slab with water to prevent the slab from leeching the water from the new cement. The process by which cement and plaster set up is chemical rather than a drying action, and if the water is removed before this reaction is complete, a weakened mixture is the result.

It's important to cover the whole area with a uniform thickness of cement, so a special serrated trowel is a must. Mix the cement in small batches to a somewhat soupy consistency, then spread it on evenly. Position the tiles, pushing them down firmly into the cement with a twisting, back-and-forth motion before aligning them with the neighboring tiles into neat rows. While the cement is still wet, check the completed rows of tile from every angle to spot any unwanted irregularities.

You usually have to wait a day or so for the tilesetting cement to cure before grouting. This is a simple, satisfying job that makes the bunch of tiles just laid suddenly look like an attractive tile floor. Mix up a soupy batch of grout in the

140

color you have chosen, wet the whole area down and then spread the grout over the whole job, working it vigorously back and forth and in circles to remove any air bubbles hiding down in the cracks between the tiles.

After you're certain that each crack is completely filled with grout, let the job sit for twenty minutes to half an hour, or however long it takes until the grout begins to show signs of hardening. Next begin wiping the surface of the tiles to wash away excess grout. Use a dampened sponge, dipping the sponge back into a bucket of water from time to time. Keep working over the surface to remove the grout from the face of the tiles, using as little water as possible to wipe away the grout without gouging it. When the face of the tile is cleaned of all lumps of grout, add just a little extra water to the sponge to help clean the face of the tiles still further and to give a smoother finish to the grout left between the tiles.

Let the tile sit for a while when the job reaches this stage. You can go over it again about an hour later to clean a little more grout from the surface if there is any left. After several hours the tile can be scrubbed harder to remove any final discoloring left on the face of the new floor area.

14

Room Dividers and
Wall Component Shelves

Room dividers can take on a number of different basic shapes, forms and functions. Some provide extra shelving and/or lighting, whereas others are built in the form of a cabinet bar to expand your eating-entertaining areas. A third type, made for the sole purpose of breaking up the room volume into smaller, more usable portions, can take the shape of a see-through grill or turned posts, or just a simple paneled or painted wall. For the sake of some sort of organization, we'll start off with the simplest and work toward the more exotic forms of dividers.

Adding a Simple Paneled Wall Room Divider

The first step is to decide what form of wall covering will best work into the design of the room. Generally you have all the wall treatments previously discussed to choose from: wood paneling, painted drywall, textured plaster over drywall, pretextured drywall, pretextured masonite, shingles over plywood, weathered lumber over plywood or even imitation brick and rock over plywood (although these last two tend to look a little less convincing on a new divider wall all by itself than they would on an existing wall). Because a new divider wall is nothing more than an afterthought, the goal is to make it blend into the surrounding room to break up the volume without clashing with the finish of the room. So, to make a room divider look more natural, an understated wall covering that blends in may be the best choice.

The backing material for all the above treatments can be plywood, masonite or gypsumboard—all of which come in 4' x 8' sheets and can be nailed to 2" x 4" studs. So, no matter which treatment you choose, the underlying framing can be much the same for all. The only reason for choosing the covering material before doing anything else is so that you can buy it first and use it as a mock-up to find the exact positioning of the wall.

Framing for the Divider Wall

Once the position of the wall has been decided upon, nail a 2" x 4" along the base of the new wall position, using large masonry nails if the wall is to be

142

placed over a slab. The 2"x 4" should be as long as the proposed wall, minus 1-5/8", and should be positioned with one end butted against the existing wall.

When the bottom 2" x 4" plate is in place (and it can rest right on top of the existing floor covering), a 2" x 4" is cut to fit between the top of the 2" x 4" plate and the ceiling, running up the wall adjacent to the divider. Using a framing level, mark the position of this upright 2" x 4", and nail it to the wall with 3" box nails. If the upright 2" x 4" doesn't happen to lie against a stud in the existing wall (and chances are it won't), it can be nailed at the very top end

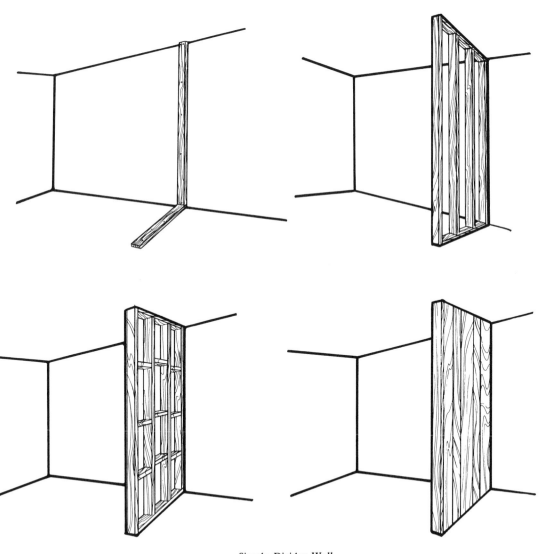

Simple Divider Wall

143

into the 2" x 4" plate running along the top of the existing wall, and into the bottom plate of the new divider wall. A couple of 1/2" holes can be drilled through the upright and through the wall, and then "blind" bolts (with nuts which have flanges that fold back and then outward when pushed through the hole) can be inserted and tightened to hold the upright firmly against the wall.

Next cut a 2" x 4" as long as the height from the floor to the ceiling. Position this vertically against the free end of the bottom plate and mark the position of its top end on the ceiling when the level shows it to be placed exactly straight up and down, viewed from both the front and side. If it is a little short and hard to hold steady enough to mark, place the bottom flush against the end of the bottom plate and sink two nails through the upright and into the end of the bottom plate. Then slide a nail or sliver of wood between the top of the upright and the ceiling to hold it in place so it can be positioned vertically.

Now cut a top plate 2" x 4" the length of the distance between the inside edges of the uprights at the bottom to use as a top plate running along the ceiling between the two uprights. The top plate is nailed into the ceiling joists, and then the top of the end upright is nailed into the end of the top plate.

Vertical studs extending from the top of the bottom plate to the bottom of the top plate should be placed within this framework at 16" intervals. If the wall is to be longer than four feet, make certain that there is a stud positioned with its center exactly four feet from the existing wall to form a backing behind the butt joint of the sheets of wall covering which will meet at that point. When the studs have been nailed in place to the top and bottom plates, cut 2" x 4" horizontal braces to be nailed between the studs about 24", 48" and 72" up from the bottom. These braces can be staggered in height somewhat so that nails can be driven through the studs and into them without being blocked by the adjoining brace.

Once this framework is solidly in place, you can attach the wall covering as described in the various wall treatment chapters. For paneled divider walls, a 4" wide cap strip can be cut from matching wood to provide an end piece for the wall. You may also want to run moldings around the wall where it meets the existing wall and ceiling.

Variations of the Divider Wall

Another variation of the nonfunctional divider wall theme is the type built of solid wall to a height of three or four feet and then continued up to the ceiling with a grating or turned posts. A framework is built in exactly the same way as for a full height divider wall, except that the uprights are shortened, of course, to provide the height of wall desired under the posts or grate. Then a 4-1/2" wide capping piece is cut from 2" stock to lie on top of the top plate. A matching capping piece is cut to fit over the top ends of the posts and against the ceiling.

The turned posts are then cut to the length of the distance from the top of the solid wall portion to the ceiling, minus the thickness of the two capping boards. If turned posts are out of the question economically, suitable substitutes can be cut from soft wood (pine, cedar or redwood) with a bandsaw. Simply draw the pattern of the post design that you like onto the right half of one side of a 4" x 4". Cut out this pattern, and then use the cut edge of the 4" x 4" as a pattern to mark the other posts. Once they have been cut on all four sides, one of them can be used to draw the pattern on the rest of the sides of the first post. The whole project does take a bit of sawwork, but the cuts are all short, there is no real need for absolute accuracy—and the resulting posts create a surprisingly attractive effect at a very small fraction of the cost of ready-made turned posts. Of course, if you are already working with a lathe, then the problem of getting long turned posts is further simplified.

Once the posts are cut, mark the center point of their positions on the centerline of the capping pieces; drill 1/4" holes through the capping boards at these points; countersink the holes; then sink 2-1/2" or 3" flathead screws through these holes and into the centers of the ends of the posts, securing them at regular intervals to both capping boards. Finally, lift the whole post assembly into position and nail down through the bottom capping board into the top plate of the solid wall frame, and up through the top capping board into the ceiling joists with 2-1/2" finishing nails. Cover the sides of the solid wall frame with the wall covering of your choice.

If any nonfunctional divider is to be less than three feet long, you may want to frame the wall out of 2" x 3"s or 2" x 2"s in order to keep the proportions of the divider to scale.

Shelf-Component Divider Walls

Thicker divider walls can be put to work as shelving units for storage and display. The shelves can be either the see-through variety or completely backed with your choice of wall treatment. As a third alternative (and perhaps the most effective), a backing can be built on one side or the other of each shelf, creating an interesting and functional solid divider wall. Of course, what is backing for a shelf on one side of the wall is a flat wall area for posters, photos, paintings or corkboards, and so forth, on the other. You have a free hand in designing not only the layout of the shelves but also the pattern of shelf and flat display area that will be visible on each side. There's nothing to prevent you from combining both backed and see-through shelves in the same divider; and even indirect lighting panels can be worked into a divider wall without much trouble.

The structural uprights and horizontal shelf areas can be cut from 1" x 10" or 1" x 12" clear stock of your favorite wood. If the shelves are to be painted, then less expensive shelving stock can be used. You can use 2" x 10" or 2" x 12" stock, of course, but it creates a heavy, bulky look from our point of view—although this is largely a matter of taste. So long as there is an upright divider-brace every thirty inches or so, or a backing behind the longer shelves (extending either up to or down from the shelf), then the 1" x 10" or 1" x 12" stock will work well at half the cost.

145

Which Type of Shelf-Component Divider Wall To Choose

Of course, there are a hundred different ways to build divider shelf units, so we'll describe the best way we've found over the years of putting up dividers and components in various shapes and sizes. That way you can get a plan of action to work from.

The first step is to lay out a scale drawing of the dimensions of the wall. Then check the shelves that already exist in the house to get an idea of what length and spacing you like and don't like. A trip to a favorite furniture store with the tape measure might be in order here if you happen to have seen a wall component unit that caught your eye. Take down the basic proportions so you'll have an idea of what to strive for in your own unit.

Then take a look at the size of the books, TV's, record players, statuary, and so forth, that you'd like the unit to house. Keeping all these dimension requirements in mind, start to lay out the shelf design of the unit by locating the vertical upright members first (usually placing them at regular intervals, creating what decorators call a "modular" design). Then work in the placement of the various shelf functions (TV shelf, magazine rack shelf, record shelf, and so forth) to suit the layout of the surrounding room. Finally, when you have an idea where the basics should go, you can fill in the rest with odd shelves and lighting to suit your fancy.

Whenever you have a combination of prominent vertical and horizontal lines, you'll end up with a very boxy, square look; so, you may want to relieve the monotony of all the straight lines and right-angle corners with a few curves—which can do much to soften the squared-off "egg crate" effect.

One way to work curves into a shelf unit design is by placing arched framing over an occasional shelf, positioned just back from the front of the unit. You may want to try sketching in an arch or two within the shelf areas to see how it would look.

Of course, a divider wall shelf unit is a bit more involved than a regular wall component unit because you have the reverse side to worry about. Try to work out a pattern for the backings of the different shelves that will create useful and interesting display areas on the reverse side of the divider—hopefully, areas that will fit into the function of the room as well. You may be faced with a compromise or two on this point, and if you have to use the same area for a shelf on both sides of the unit, you can either omit the backing from that particular one to make it a see-through space, or you can place the backing on the lengthwise centerline of the shelf, creating a narrower one on both sides with a solid backing.

Construction of the Shelf-Component Divider Wall

The basic construction plan is to run a number of floor-to-ceiling divider supports (about three for a four-foot-wide unit, four for a six- to ten-foot unit, and so on), using these supports to carry the horizontal shelves and their backing and possibly an occasional arch or smaller lighting shelf.

Once you have the number of board feet figured for the project, keep the use of the different boards in mind as they're picked from the lumber pile. If the unit is to be stained or varnished, make certain you get enough boards with interesting grain to form the most prominent uprights. One of the uprights will be against the existing wall, of course, so it can be flawed on one side. But the rest will be displayed quite openly, so make sure you get good, unblemished, dry boards. Most of the shelves will be covered with books and bric-a-brac, so you can accept less interesting boards for shelf use, with the exception of the angled magazine rack shelf, which will be displaying its grain.

Due to the relatively large area of board feet needed for the shelf units, most expensive hardwoods are out of the question for the average budget. However, clear fir or redwood can both be stained—at a saving—to create a warm, inviting look. Pine is suitable for painted shelving, but it has a very flat, dull appearance when stained.

Once you have the lumber home, take another careful look at it and arrange the boards in order, with the best ones at one end, progressing down to the worst-looking on the other. The best board usually becomes the vertical end piece, and the worst boards can be used for shelving.

Now measure the exact distance from the ceiling to the floor at each point where an upright will be positioned. You have a rare house if all the measurements are the same. Most structures have a combination of sagging floors and ceilings that leave you with big gaps hanging out if all the uprights are cut to the same length.

Cut the uprights the proper lengths and stand them up in place to get an approximate idea of how the positioning will work out in actual practice. Stuff match books in between the tops of the uprights and the ceiling to hold them in place until you can step back and study the effect. When you've settled on the spacing of the uprights, measure the lengths of the shelves between each pair of uprights and make out a schedule of the lengths needed: so many shelves X inches long, so many shelves Y inches long, and so forth. Mark off the lengths on the remaining lumber, making sure you're getting the most from every board. If you seem to have a lot left over, see whether you can't combine the different lengths in a way to get more shelving per board out of your lumber.

The one crucial step in making shelf units is to get all the shelves that are to be of the same dimension cut exactly square and exactly the same length. So it's a good idea to mark the lengths carefully and use a framing square to mark the cuts across the boards.

Everyone usually finds a certain saw that he works best with to get straight cuts. Whether you use a crosscut handsaw or an electric radial arm saw (ideal for this one type of cut), follow the lines as best you can. Stack all the shelves to be placed between the same two uprights on end, on a flat surface, side by side; check that none of them is more than 1/8" longer than any of the others. If they seem to be a bit off, stack them on top of one another, line them up at one end, and cut them off all at once. You may lose 1/4" or 1/2" of shelf space, but the assembly step will be much easier later on.

If a certain shelf is designed to continue along at the same height on both sides of an upright, you may want to make things still easier in assembly by simply cutting a notch in the back edge of the upright, and a notch in the front edge of the shelf where they cross each other, so they can be fitted together with these notches interlocking.

Experiment to see how the layout of the horizontal shelving works out in practice. Once you've settled on a layout, make a small mark where the shelving is to butt against the uprights and then take the uprights down.

Since the shelves are to be level, the position of the butt joint will fall at the same distance from the floor for the uprights at both ends of a shelf. So place both uprights on the floor side by side, lined up at the bottom end (making sure that the side of the upright that is showing is the side that should be joined to the shelves). Then use the framing square to mark a line across both uprights showing where the top surface of each shelf will come. Mark lines with the square 3/4" down from these first lines to show where the bottom surfaces of the shelves will be positioned (using both the top and bottom lines will save much confusion later on).

When the butt joint positions for all the shelves are marked on the uprights, the screw guide holes can be drilled through the uprights. For each butt joint, there should be three screws running through the adjoining upright and into the end grain of the shelf. The two outside holes should be positioned 2" in from the edges of the upright and centered between the two shelf positioning lines, and the middle hole should be positioned where the centerline of the upright board crosses the centerline between the shelf positioning lines.

Nails can be used to assemble a shelf unit that is secured to a solid wall, but we've found that screws are easier to work with in the long run. It takes longer to sink each screw than it does to drive a nail, but the very speed and noise of nailing seem to rush the whole job to the point where mistakes start to creep in. By the time you get the final joint nailed together, it's not uncommon to find that you've knocked the first joints loose again. Screws are easier on the whole project as it passes through the critical process of taking shape. And you'll more than likely find that they're easier on the builder as well—making the whole assembly job more calm and relaxed (and allowing the joints to be taken apart easily if a mistake *does* somehow mysteriously creep in).

Number 8, flathead wood screws, 1-1/2" long, are a good, all-around size for building shelf units. To cover up the heads, a 3/8" diameter hole can be drilled down over the 1/8" screw-guide holes to hide the screwheads. The guide holes should be drilled all the way through the uprights, of course, whereas the countersink holes should be only about 1/2" to 3/8" deep, or about halfway through the board.

After the screw-guide holes have all been drilled through the uprights, drill the countersink holes, making sure to check that they are drilled into the side of the upright opposite from the butt-joint positioning lines. If two shelves butt on both sides of the same upright at exactly the same level (and if you've decided not to notch the shelving and the uprights together at this crossing point), attach one of the shelves in the normal way. Then angle screw-guide holes up from this shelf, through the upright and into the end of the other shelf positioned at the same level.

When the screw-guide holes and countersink holes have been drilled in the uprights, you can begin to position the uprights permanently. You may want to stain or varnish the wood before putting it up and assembling the unit. By doing the finishing first, you can obviously do it where the spills won't matter and the fumes won't get to you—and where the boards are much easier to reach. But some builders maintain that if you finish the unit after it has been assembled, you get a slightly nicer color effect at the joints and corners where the stain is usually left a little darker, helping to hide minor mistakes, and creating a more antiqued and established appearance.

Assembling can begin by fastening the anchoring end piece to the wall. You may have to cut away a molding along the bottom of the adjoining wall where the upright overlaps it. Mark the position of both edges of the upright on the molding, and then cut the molding through at these spots with a hammer and wood chisel.

With the upright sitting against the wall, mark its position, using a level to make certain the edges are straight up and down. Then check the wall behind the area to be covered by the upright to see whether there might be a wall stud hidden behind the wall covering. If so, the upright can be anchored in position with 2-1/2" or 3" finishing nails running through the upright and into the stud. If not, the upright can be nailed at the extreme top and bottom, angling the nails through the upright and into the top and bottom plates along the wall.

Before nailing the upright into position, however, the shelving should be joined to the upright with the screws and white glue spread along the end grain of the shelves.

Assembling wall component or shelf dividers is "when a feller needs a friend"—to hold up the other end of the shelves and to generally steady the whole assembly, not to mention the assembler.

To assemble, prop up the upright about two feet out from its position on the wall and attach the bottom shelf to it with screws and glue. Then attach the other end of the shelf to the next upright. Next attach the top shelf to both uprights, and then any others that are also to be attached to the two uprights.

When this first unit is assembled, it can be moved over into position against the wall and nailed or screwed to the existing wall. To put up the next unit, the shelves extending from the last upright to the next can be screwed and glued in place to the next upright, lying on its edge on the floor. Then the single upright with shelves attached can be carefully lifted up and the free ends of the shelves attached to the upright already standing anchored. In this way you can keep on adding modular shelf units, or whatever you want to call them, as far as you want the divider to extend.

When all the uprights are in place, use the level to line them up vertically; mark their vertical positions on the ceiling, and then angle finishing nails up through the top ends of the uprights into the ceiling, just to hold the unit up straight until the top molding is attached.

When the whole unit is in place, the backings for the shelves, cut from additional shelving stock, can be put in place and nailed or screwed so that the backside of the backing is inset about 1/4" from the surrounding uprights and shelving to form a framework for the backing. If corkboard is to be placed over the backing, then the backing can be inset the thickness of the cork, plus 1/2", to form a natural frame around the cork panel.

Narrower, incidental shelves or lighting frameworks can also be added at this time. Then a 2" wide cornice board can be run around the very top of the divider, pushed up solidly against the ceiling and then nailed into the fronts of the uprights. If this cornice is snug against the ceiling, the divider unit will not be able to budge in any direction.

When all the incidentals and accessories have been added to your divider unit, cut a handful of plugs from a 3/8" diameter dowel on the bandsaw, table saw, or with a hacksaw; make each plug about 1/4" to 3/8" long. Then grab a squeeze bottle of white glue, a mallet or hammer, and fill the countersink holes with the dowel plugs. Place a dab of white glue in each hole, put the plug just in the hole, and then tap it in until it's flush with the surface of the wood.

Any shelving space to be enclosed can be covered with doors made from additional wood stock, as shown in the illustrations. Look for hidden cabinet hinges for the doors in the hardware section of the local supply yard. These are easier to mount and give the unit a well-finished look. If you'd like to avoid using conspicuous-looking handles on such wood panel doors, you can make use of touch latches which spring the door open when given a slight push.

You may also want to cover one of the waist-high shelves so that it can be used as a serving bar or buffet for entertaining. There are a number of effective ways to cover a simple shelf-bar that will greatly enhance the looks and versatility of the unit. Cutting an enlarged front edge-border for the shelf will allow you to cover the shelf itself with laminated plastic veneer, tile, leather-like material, glass, fiberglass, or a number of other waterproof, stainproof surfaces. Make an edging for the front of the bar with a strip of matching wood stock to cover the rough edge of this surface.

Sand the whole shelf unit thoroughly and finish—if this step hasn't already been taken care of.

Wall Component Shelves

Wall components can be made in exactly the same way as the room divider shelf units, except that you don't have two exposed sides to worry about—and you can brace up a long shelf that might sag under the weight of books and the like, using cleats or 3/4" x 3/4" battens nailed into the wall just under the shelf.

15

Closets and Dressing Table Areas

In most houses some extra square footage devoted to closets wouldn't hurt. If you have any plans for converting a spare room into another bedroom, the closet-building project is a must in most cases.

Any blank wall can be a candidate for a new closet layout. And while we're at it, we might as well cover the whole area with an interesting wall texture, and possibly build in an adjoining dressing table area to cover the whole wall without much added effort.

Planning the Closet

The first step in building new closets is to check the existing closets in the house. This will give you a clear idea of exactly how deep and how long you think the ideal closet should be. If the ones you look at are perfectly suitable, you can copy their dimensions; but if they somehow miss the mark, you'll know what mistakes to avoid. So look them all over to get an idea of where to start laying out the new project.

There are any number of good ways to build closets, but we'll describe one method that has proved quite dependable over the years. The basic scheme is to build a simple 2" x 4" framing to enclose the closet box and provide a place to hang the closet door(s) and clothes hanger pole(s) and shelves. Then this framework is covered with a wall covering you like, and the door(s) hung.

Before drawing up the plans for the framework, you may also want to look around at the various types of closet doors available. These can range from simple hollow-core sliding or hinged doors to shutter doors, bifold (double-folding) doors, bifold mirror doors or ordinary paneled closet doors. The reason to check the doors you like at this stage of the game is to find out what range of sizes is available in the styles you like; then you can design the door opening dimensions with this in mind.

For the sake of an example, we'll give the steps and dimensions needed to make the double closet-cum-dressing-table area pictured in the illustration. Then, if you need only a smaller portion of the unit, it will be a simple matter to reduce the recipe to suit the closet to your needs.

Bedroom Closet

Framing the Closet

First cut four 2" x 4"'s to run vertically at the four corners of the closet box from the floor to the ceiling. Next, to form an overall depth of 24" in the closet, cut four 20-3/4" lengths of 2" x 4". These will be nailed at the top and bottom between the two uprights at both ends. Nail these rectangular frames together and then nail one of the uprights of each frame to the wall in position, checking with a framing level to make certain the upright is vertical. You may have to cut away the molding along the bottom of the existing wall with a hammer and chisel to allow the upright to sit against the wall. If there isn't a stud behind the uprights to nail into, angle long nails (3" box nails) down through the bottom corner of the upright and into the plate running along the bottom of the existing wall; run more nails up through the top corner of the upright and into the top plate of the existing wall.

When the uprights of the two end wall frames of the closet are nailed to the wall vertically, use the framing square to position the bottom plate of the end wall frames perpendicular to the existing wall. Nail these in place to the floor. Repeat this process with the top plates of the end wall frames.

Next cut a 2" x 4" to run along the ceiling between the tops of the uprights at the corners of the end wall frames. Make certain this board is unwarped before nailing it through the ceiling and into the ceiling joists.

Cut a second 2" x 4" to a length equaling that of the 2" x 4" just cut, *plus* 7". Mark two lines across this board, 3-1/2" in from both ends. Next mark a line 1-5/8" in from one side edge of the 2" x 4", extending from the lines just

drawn to the ends of the board, parallel to the side edge. Now cut out the 3-1/2" x 1-5/8" notches marked on the same side edge at both ends of the 2" x 4". This board is to be nailed to the backsides of the upright corner posts of the closet box. The board should be positioned so that the notches cut in its edge at the ends fit over the back of both uprights, and the front edge of the 2" x 4" is flush with the front side of the uprights. Before nailing, mark the uprights, measuring up from the floor the height of the doors you plan to use, *plus* 1/2". Now the notched 2" x 4" header piece can be nailed to the backsides of the uprights with its bottom side positioned at this mark.

Measure the distance from the bottom of the 2" x 4" running along the ceiling between the two uprights, down to the top of the header board above the door(s). Then cut enough 2" x 4"s to this length to be able to place one vertically between the ceiling 2" x 4" and the headboard every 16". Measure over from the outside of either corner upright 16" and make a mark on the header board; then do the same on the ceiling board. Next nail one of the short 2" x 4" pieces between these two boards with the marks positioned along the centerline of the edge of the 2" x 4". Measure over another 16" and place another short 2" x 4" in position in the same way—and so on across the front of the closet box.

Next measure the width of each door (or set of doors) for each opening; add 1/2"; then measure in from the inside of the adjacent corner upright along the header board and mark the width of the door opening on the header board. For single door openings, simply measure the overall width of the front of the closet box and make a mark at the center point on the header board. Then measure the width of the door(s); add 1/2"; divide this number by two; measure out from the center point on both sides to this distance and make a mark.

Measure the distance from the floor to the bottom of the header board and then cut a 2" x 4" to this length for each double door opening (two for a single door opening). These door frames can be nailed vertically to the outside of the marks showing the position of the door openings, running from the bottom side of the header board down to the floor. Use the level to make sure the door frames are vertical.

The last step in the framing of the closet box is to cut six more short pieces of 2" x 4" equal to the length of the plates between the uprights at the corners of the closet. Position these braces horizontally between the front and back uprights on each end wall at heights of two, four and six feet. You can nail cleats to the uprights immediately below the brace positions to make the nailing a little easier and more solid.

Wall Covering for the Closet

The time has come to start enclosing the structure. Whatever type of wall sheeting you have decided on, start out by ripping two of the sheets right down the center line. Nail one of the half-sheets to each of the outside end walls;

then nail the other two half-sheets to the insides of the end wall frames (after cutting a 1-5/8" x 3-1/2" notch in both inside sheets to fit around the header board).

Next lay the remaining wall covering in place against the front of the closet; from the backside draw the outline of the door openings on the back of the sheet, making sure the sheet of wall covering is exactly in position.

Cut out the door openings and nail up the wall covering, making certain that a vertical frame is positioned behind the butt joint if there is to be more than one sheet put up.

Shelves and Poles

The next step is to put up the clothes hanger poles and the shelf for hats, shoes, and so forth. You can find 1-1/4" and 1-3/8" diameter dowels at the lumberyard that are made for just this purpose. If you happen to have a length of 1" or more diameter pipe lying about, you can make use of this instead and avoid the sag that sometimes results when you hang too many coats on a wooden clothes pole. Just be sure not to use a rod whose diameter is too large for a hanger to fit on.

If the closet is a single door type, simply cut two 2" x 4"s to fit between the back of the front wall of the closet box and the existing wall, running horizontally along the insides of the end walls. When these are measured and cut, drill a hole for the clothes pole through the exact center point of the two 2" x 4"s. Cut the hanger pole to the distance between the insides of the end walls. Then, with the framing square, draw a horizontal line across the insides of the end walls, five feet up from the floor. Insert the hanger pole through the holes in the 2" x 4"s and nail the 2" x 4"s to the framing of the end walls, positioned with their bottom edges along the horizontal lines.

With a double-door opening closet, use the level to draw a horizontal line on the existing wall directly behind the center divider between the two sets of doors, five feet from the floor. Draw more lines at the same level, one inside each end wall, and one on the back of the framing of the center divider of the front wall. Cut and drill the two end wall clothes pole 2" x 4" supports exactly as completed in the single door closet. Then cut a short length of 2" x 4" to fit between the two upright door frames in the center of the closet front wall. Cut and drill two more clothes pole supports from 2" x 4" stock to fit between the existing wall and the back of the front wall covering, between the two upright center door frames. Also, cut a piece of 1" x 4", 24" long. Cut two lengths of clothes pole, as long as the distance from the insides of the end walls to the center of the closet, minus 1".

Nail the end wall pole supports into the framing of the end walls with their bottom edges lying along the horizontal marker line. Nail the short length of 2" x 4" between the center upright door frames with its *top* edge lying along the horizontal marker line. Next find the positions of two studs in the existing wall just below the horizontal line on the existing wall, and nail the 1" x 4" solidly to these studs with its *top* edge lying along the marker line, centered behind the divider. This cleat must be attached firmly to the existing wall framing, so make sure the nails grab something solid when they go in.

Now the two center pole supports can be drilled with a hole through each, 12" from the end of the support that will be butted back against the existing wall. Insert the pole in the end wall support; slip the center support over the other end, and set one end of the center pole support down on top of the cleat running along the existing wall. Place the other end on top of the short 2" x 4" extending between the center upright door frames, and nail in place. Repeat this to mount the other hanger pole in the same way.

The shelf over the poles should be mounted on top of 1" x 1" spacers to raise the bottom of it up over the clothes pole high enough to allow hangers to be hooked on the pole without any obstruction. Rip a 1" x 1" batten to fit on top of each clothes pole support and then nail these in place.

Next rip two lengths of 1" x 8" to fit with their ends sitting flat on top of the 1" x 1" spacers, side by side. Cut one pair of shelf boards for each pair of hanger pole supports, and simply nail in place on top of the spacers.

Hanging the Doors

Once the shelf and poles are in place, the hanging of the doors and the wall covering finish work can be carried out. The doors can be hung on standard butt hinges, with magnetic latches mounted to the bottom of the header boards for standard doors. Bifold, accordion and sliding doors will have their own mounting tracks supplied with them.

Practically any type of wooden door, including shutters, can be cut off, or added to, to fill out a suitably large door opening. If you find shutters or old double doors that aren't quite wide enough, remember that an inch or so can be added quite unobtrusively to both sides of each door or shutter from matching wood stock. This gives you four extra inches of width for the whole opening, and if that's not enough, stationary battens of matching wood can also be affixed to the surrounding framing.

Dressing Table Areas

If an adjoining dressing table area is to be built next to the closet to carry the new look along the whole wall (creating a handy area in the bedroom at the same time), the new covering can be continued all the way along the existing wall. Then a short divider extending out from the existing wall can be framed up exactly like one of the end walls of the closet (except that the framing should be made from 2" x 2" stock to keep the proportions reduced, considering the shallow overall depth of the new divider wall).

A 1" x 2" cap board can be ripped to cover the end of the wall. A typical dressing table area enclosure such as this will usually vary in width from about 24" to 48", although the actual limits are set only by your own wants and the length of the existing wall.

The counter can be set at about 30" from the floor if it's to be used as a dressing table with a chair; or at about 36" to 40" if used as a stand-up counter aid for hair arranging and so on. Use the level to draw a horizontal line on all three sides of the area, 1-5/8" below the countertop height desired. Nail inside corner molding around the three sides with a flat edge to the top, aligned with the marker line. Then two 2" x 12"s can be cut to fit between the divider wall and the end wall of the closet and up against the existing wall.

These boards can be covered with a number of suitable countertop surfaces: laminated plastic veneer, tiles, linoleum, cork tiles, leatherette; or simply stain or fiber-glass the boards themselves if they have an attractive grain pattern. For ways to mount the various countertops, consult the chapter on countertops which goes into the various processes in depth.

16

Bathroom Divider Walls
and Pullman Counters

A pullman counter which fills in around the rather unfinished bottoms of sinks can do more to pull all the areas of a bathroom together into a central design theme than any other bathroom project. Not only does a pullman cabinet cover the traditionally ugly areas of the room but also it can provide a great deal of added storage space. There are some technical points to keep in mind when planning one, however. So if you're not up on the dos and don'ts of plumbing as well as you might be, it's a good idea to check over the construction sections dealing with toilets and sinks before settling on a plan of action. Just a quick run-through will give you enough background so that you can start laying plans.

Planning the Counter and Divider Walls

Basically there are two types of pullmans that lend themselves to solving the problems of a dull bathroom: those that create a counter which flows around the sink area and on over the tank of the toilet with a single, unbroken countertop; and those that make use of divider walls to break up the areas, providing separate enclosures for the toilet and sink areas.

The latter is better suited to breaking up the monotony of a larger bathroom (or re-creating a completely new bathroom to hook up to the old drain pipes), whereas the former can do more to help out a smaller bathroom, especially if the old fixtures are to be left in place.

As in every room project, the first step is to take a close look at what you have to work with. Check both the shape and condition of the fixtures. As we've mentioned earlier, the vast majority of bathrooms are planned around the most expedient plumbing layout possible rather than any preconceived visual design of the fixture arrangement.

The plumbing hook-ups are usually all along one wall, and the usual positioning of fixtures as you enter the room is: toilet-sink-tub. Even if you have a more unusual plumbing arrangement, you can make modifications in this pullman theme that will suit your conditions. We'll take a look at the step-by-step methods used to convert a typical bathroom into the combination divider wall/pullman counter as shown in the illustrations. Then the changes

158

needed to produce a variation perfectly suited to your needs will become a little more obvious.

Taking Stock of the Fixtures

If you're on a limited budget, and the toilet isn't too badly worn, perhaps the best idea is to figure a way to cover its flaws and use it as is. With a new seat and a built-in cover shelf over the tank, it will look nearly as good as a new one. Except in cases in which the toilet is in pretty sad shape, you don't gain a lot visually by putting in a new unit.

With sinks, the situation is reversed. The sink is the least expensive fixture in the whole bathroom, and as most older sinks are of the wall-hung variety, you'll gain a lot of visual improvement for your dollar by investing in a counter-mounted sink to use with the new pullman.

With tubs, the same situation exists as with toilets. A brand-new one won't do too much to change the concept of the room layout, and considering the cost and effort demanded by a tub change, it's worth it only in extreme cases. The exception to this is if you plan to replace the tub with a shower enclosure, which can do much to update a bathroom, provide added floor space and change the whole visual impact of the room.

The cost is relatively high for such a project, and almost the same effect can be created a lot more cheaply and easily by simply making a shower enclosure out of the tub area. Opaque sliding glass doors can be mounted on a tub in a matter of minutes.

For the purposes of the bathroom in our example, we'll discard the old sink but make the best of the toilet and tub with a few well-placed modifications. Also to go are the spartan mirror cabinet and wall-mounted light just above it, which are found in most bathrooms. These are usually in pretty poor shape after a few years' use and are of questionable appeal at their best.

Preparation

Since the wall behind the fixtures will generally be given a new treatment as well, a simple place to start the rebuilding process is to rip out the molding along the bottom. Even if you're planning on wallpapering or painting, a nice wide (3/4" x 2-1/2") batten used for bottom molding will give a fresh, new border to the paper or paint (trimmed in a color to match the fixtures). When you're warmed up a bit, the next step is to remove the shelves from the mirror cabinet and unscrew the mounting screws from the inner side walls so that the cabinet can be taken out.

Next make certain that no electric current is going to the light; then remove the fixture, wrapping tape around the exposed wire ends for now. If you do a lot of your work at night, of course, skip this step until later. Once you're rolling nicely, you can start to remove the sink.

Shut off the hot and cold water at the taps below the sink. While you're at it, check the condition of these taps. If they show signs of corrosion or cracking, this is a good time to replace them. The steps for all plumbing tasks

THE ART OF MAKING HOUSES LIVEABLE

Pullman Cabinet

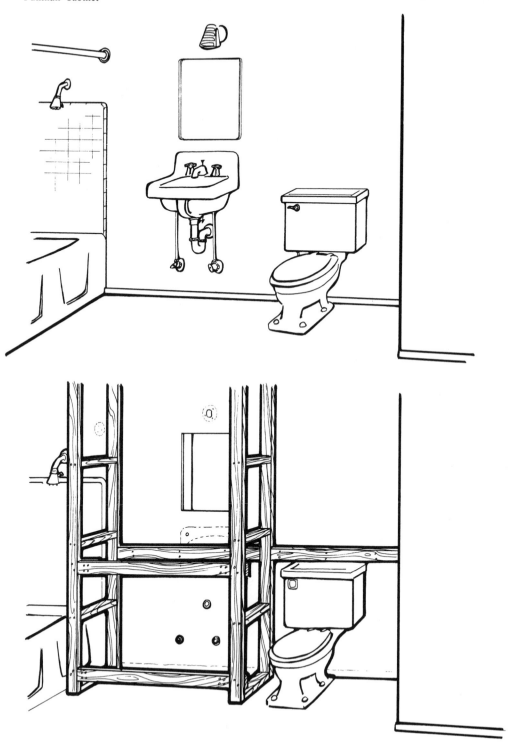

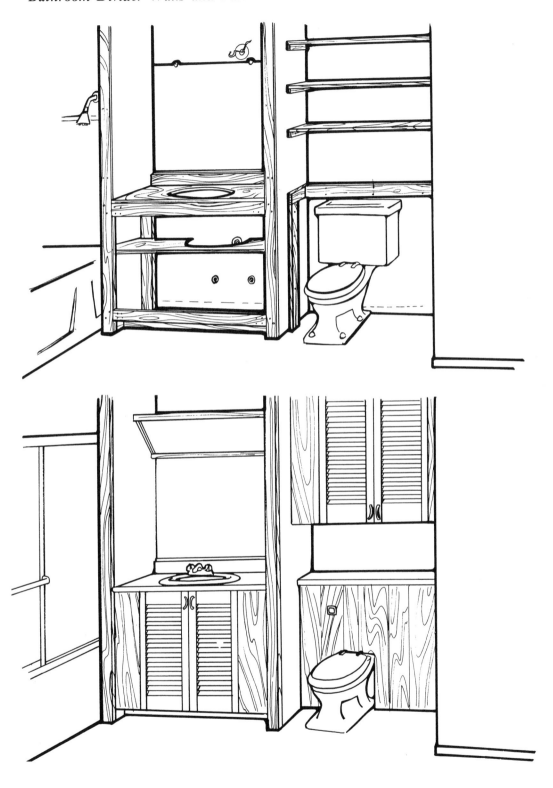

are to be found in the plumbing chapter (oddly enough)—and if you're a little rusty in your wrench techniques, it may be a good idea to review the steps quickly before forging ahead and damaging the system back in the wall where you can't get at it. Loosen the drain where the vertical pipe enters the U-shaped trap.

Once the inlet tubes are loosened and the drain is free, some sinks will lift right off a cast iron mounting flange screwed to the wall. Others may have screws or bolts passing through a flange in the sink itself. Whatever the case, it's usually a self-evident mount that holds the sink to the wall and little expertise is needed to carry out this step.

Unless there is something of special interest about the faucets, the whole sink assembly can usually be discarded without any great loss. There may be some drainpipes which look to be in good condition, but you're better off spending the little extra to start over with all-new plumbing hook-ups.

Framing the Pullman and Divider Walls

According to the schedule, you should be ready to start framing the pullman and the divider walls at about this stage of the game. From the plumbing chapter you will glean a few points about choosing the sink and the countertop surface together so that their methods of mounting will be compatible. Look over the choices at the lumberyard or in catalogues to get an idea of a general size to build the counter (if you don't already have a sink). Eighteen inches is an average fore-and-aft diameter of a countertop sink; and after the framing is in place, the counter will usually measure around twenty-two inches from the edge to the back wall.

Cut four uprights from *straight* construction grade fir 2" x 4"s to form the vertical members of the two divider walls, reaching from the floor to the ceiling. Then cut eight horizontal braces to run between the two uprights in both walls, the length of the depth of the counter, minus 3-1/4" (or 18-3/4" in this example). Cut three 2" x 4"s the length of the distance between the two divider walls.

Place all four uprights on the floor, flat side up, and use the framing square to make a mark squarely across all four boards at distances of 24", 48" and 72", measuring from one end.

Next make a ladder framework for both walls. Place one of the cross members flush with the end of an upright, and sink two nails through the upright and into the end grain of the cross member. Repeat this until there are four cross members nailed at 24" intervals between each pair of uprights.

Stand one of the divider wall frames in place vertically, within an inch or so of the tub, and nail into the wall with 2-1/2" or 3" box nails. If the nails don't hit a stud, angle two up into the top corner of the frame and then two more down through the bottom corner of the frame so that the nails sink into the top and bottom plates of the existing wall.

Use the boards which were cut to fit between the divider walls to measure the position of the other wall frame and, using a level, mark this position.

162

Then tilt the frame up and nail it in place against the wall in the same manner as the first wall.

Use a level or framing square to mark the base level for the countertop on the existing wall, then locate the wall studs and nail one of the 2" x 4"s to the wall, sinking the nails *firmly* into the studs. Measure the distance from the floor up to the level of the countertop base and mark this level on the inside edges of the two wall uprights closest to you. Nail cleats to the back of another of the cut 2" x 4"s at both ends, then nail through these cleats and into the uprights to position the 2" x 4" flush with the front of the uprights and with the top edge at the level of the base of the countertop. Nail the same cleats to the ends of the last cut 2" x 4", then nail this also flush with the front of the uprights, parallel to the floor, and with its bottom edge about 3-1/2" from the floor. Use some scrap 2" x 4"s on edge to space the board up from the floor.

Covering the Framing

The time has come to start putting a surface on all this framing. So, whether you're putting up paneling, drywall to be painted or 1/4" plywood as a base for wallpaper or special effect textures, cut two 22" x 96" pieces to be nailed to the outsides of both divider walls (with 2" finishing nails). Next cut two pieces of sheeting to fit on the inside surfaces of the divider walls, extending from the counter base level up to the ceiling. If paneling is to be used, cut an additional piece to cover the wall that will mount the mirror, between the two divider walls, extending up from the counter base level to the ceiling. Cut a hole in the paneling above the proposed height of the new mirror to allow the wiring for the lights to be threaded through.

If paneling is the choice for wall covering, continue to cover the remaining portion of the wall. Cut the shape of the countertop from 5/8" or 3/4" exterior plywood to rest on top of the two 2" x 4"s, extending across between the uprights of the divider walls. Mark the most logical center point for the new sink on top of the counter wood. If a cutout pattern is not supplied with the sink, then cut a hole out of a sheet of corrugated plywood that is big enough to allow a flat mounting of the sink. Position this pattern squarely over the marked center point and draw the outline onto the countertop wood.

Cut the hole for the sink with a keyhole saw or electric saber saw by drilling a 1/2" starter hole in the cutout area and working your way around the outline from there. Check both the sink and countertop chapters to adapt the sequence of work steps to your choice of sink mountings and countertop surfaces. If tile is used, the sink can be mounted at this point after nailing down the counter base. The steps for hooking up a new sink to the pipes can be found in the plumbing chapter.

Covering the Toilet

To build a counter that covers the back of the toilet, measure the distance from the front of the tank (without the tank cover) to the wall. Nail a vertical 2" x 4" on the divider wall next to the toilet and on the opposite existing wall, extending up from the floor to the height of the bottom of the sink base. Nail a horizontal 2" x 4" cleat along the wall behind the toilet with its top edge at the same level as the bottom of the counter base. Nail a second horizontal brace to fit between the vertical 2" x 4"s, flush with their top ends and front sides. This can be cut from 2" x 4" stock in many cases, but the height of the counter, as well as the height and shape of the toilet tank, will sometimes dictate using a smaller front horizontal brace.

Cut a sheet of the wall covering as wide and as long as the covering panel in front of the toilet tank; then cut a notch the width and height of the seat base so that the panel can be slipped down over the front of the tank with its back surface against the front of the tank.

The best way to bring the toilet handle forward through the covering panel is to replace the traditional handle with a push-button unit, available at most lumber and supply yards.

A hole can then be cut in the panel for the tank-mounted button to show through, using a keyhole saw (after drilling a starter hole). There are times when a hole for the old handle can be cut through the new covering material to allow the handle to be used if desired.

After the button has been installed, and the covering panel nailed in place, cut a toilet cover countertop base from the same plywood used for the sink counter. This piece should overlap the front of the covering panel 1/2". The counter piece must be left free so that the insides of the tank can be serviced easily. Finish the top of the cover to match the rest of the pullman counter.

Indirect Lighting

To make indirect lighting, first mount two simple porcelain light sockets on the wall about 3" to 4" above the proposed top edge of the mirror. *Making certain that the current is off,* splice on an extension of one of the wire ends, running the extension onto one of the connecting screws of both sockets. Then splice on another extension to the other wire, and attach it to the other connecting screws in the same way. Screw in the bulbs and make certain they work before moving on to the building of the light frame.

One way to build a lighting frame (as shown) is to cut off a length of 1" x 12" stock, 11-1/2" long. Make a mark on one side 2" from one end. Then on the opposite side, make another mark 2" from the opposite end and draw a straight line diagonally across the board, connecting these marks which divide the board into two equal, roughly triangular shapes. These pieces will form the ends of the light cover frame. They will fit against the insides of the divider walls, with their bottom edges angling up toward the front as shown. If the ends of the light unit are to be free-standing (away from the divider wall), cut two 1" x 2" frame pieces to fit between the ends, nailed to the ends and to the existing wall.

To provide a mount for the opaque glass, or translucent white plastic light panel, use a table saw, Skilsaw or crosscut handsaw to cut a groove about 3/8" deep, 1/2" in from the angled-up edge of the end frame. The groove should be cut with two passes of the saw, making it wide enough to fit around the edge of the glass or plastic. Cut a 2" wide top frame batten from clear wood stock to a length equal to the distance between the divider walls. Next cut a 3/4" x 3/4" batten as long as the first one, minus 1-1/2".

To assemble the lighting frame, nail the end pieces against the divider walls, as shown. Then nail the inner batten to the wall (running between the end pieces of the frame and flush with them at the bottom). Cut a piece of either opaque glass or translucent plastic sheeting (available at lumberyards) to the length of the distance between the depth of the facing grooves in the end frames, and as wide as the length of the grooves from the near end to the 3/4" square batten at the other end.

Slip this light panel material into the grooves and then nail the 2" wide batten to the front edges of the end pieces, flush at the top.

If it's difficult to find the right texture of opaque glass to fit your purpose, oriental rice paper (available at art supply stores) can be cut to fit and placed on the backside of a clear glass panel to create a suitable lighting effect.

When the light frame is in place, you can install the mirror, using the steps described in the chapter on mirrors.

Light Panel

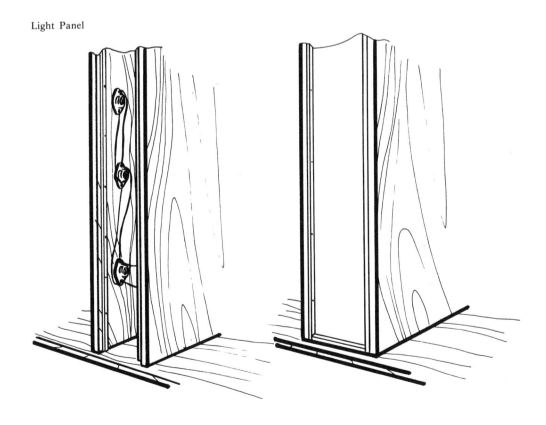

165

Finishing Up

Cut a 1" x 2" batten to fit between the two divider walls at the back of the counter as a splashboard, and nail it in place against the back wall on the countertop. At this point the countertop surfaces can be laid. All the instructions are in the following chapter. The sink can be installed and hooked into the plumbing if the sink is to fit down over the surfacing material. If laminated plastic veneer is the choice, either you can take the countertops themselves to a cabinet shop for veneering or you can cut the shapes yourself from the veneer and then cut wood (or wood-grain vinyl-coated) moldings to form a front edge for the counters.

Cut floor-to-ceiling end cap boards for the divider walls from a 4" or 4-1/2" wide wood stock to match the decorative style of the bathroom.

You can arrange the cabinet doors practically any way you like, hanging from one to four doors on the front of the cabinet. The variation shown can be made simply by nailing shutters to the center of the panel and then hinging plywood-backed, paneled doors at either end of the front panel.

Cabinets

A solution to the bathroom cabinet question is to build a separate wooden cabinet in the blank space above the counter behind the toilet. Shelving can be cut to fit on the back wall extending from the divider wall to the corner of the bathroom. Cleats can be cut from 1" x 1" stock nailed into the studs of the surrounding walls to support the shelves. Then a combination of doors can be made to match the cabinet doors used under the sink cabinet as shown.

Another, perhaps easier, way to build cabinets for this purpose is to build a ladder framework of shelving with end boards (much as for a small wall component) to fit in between the surrounding walls.

Cut the number of shelves desired from 1" x 8" or 1" x 10" stock the length of the distance between the surrounding end walls, minus 1-1/2". Then cut two end pieces to the height of the cabinet and mark the levels at which the shelves are to be joined to the end pieces, using a framing square. Drill 1/8" starter holes for screws so that the shelves can be screwed to the end pieces at these positions. Attach the shelves to the end pieces with 1-1/4" flathead, number 8 wood screws and glue, then position the entire unit and nail through the end pieces and into the framework at the corners of the surrounding end walls with 2-1/2" finishing nails. Cut two 1" x 3" pieces of stock to run up both sides of the front of the shelves, extending from the ceiling down to the bottom of the unit. Then the cabinet doors of your choice can be hinged to these end mounting boards.

17

Countertops

Although there are a number of fairly recent additions to the countertop choices available to you, the two most frequently encountered surfaces for use in kitchens and bathrooms are tile and laminated plastic veneer. There are a couple of different ways to approach both of these choices according to what you already have covering the counters.

Preparation for Replacing Tile

To replace existing tile with new tile is a fairly straightforward process. The object of the game is to remove the old tile while disturbing the old cement backing as little as possible. To do this, use a hammer and either an old wood chisel or an old cold chisel or large screwdriver to lift up the old tile. Tap the edge pieces on their bottom lips until they begin to loosen and remove all the outside corner edge pieces one by one. Always wear glasses or goggles or some sort of protective covering for your eyes when knocking tile loose from its base.

Begin lifting the surface tiles by driving the chisel under the exposed edge of the tile and gently lifting it free. When all the old tile is up, fill in any dents or holes in the old backing with grout or cement. Lay the tiles out in place and cut any border pieces needed to fill out the area. Then remove the tiles systematically and place them to one side. Next clean away all the loose dust and dirt from the surface and wet it down well to prevent leeching of the water by the new cement.

Laying the Tile

Mix up the tilesetting cement and spread it on about a two-to-three-foot-square area, using a notched trowel especially made for this purpose. The larger, square tiles often have spacer flanges (that will be covered by the grout later on) which keep the individual pieces spaced at even intervals. The smaller tiles (both the square ones and the more ornate shapes) come on one-foot-square backing sheets and can thus be laid down one square foot at a time with great ease. The backing keeps the tiles spaced at equal intervals.

With the more exotically shaped Spanish and Mediterranean types of tile, there are two kinds of half-tiles needed to bring the sheets of tiling up against the surrounding borders of the counter: those that cut each tile piece in half *across* the row of tiles, and those that cut each piece in half down the *middle* of a row of tiles. One obviously is used for the front and back edges of the tile pattern where it meets the edges of the counter; the other is to run along the side edges of the pattern to fill out the tile to the side borders.

So once the tiles have been laid down in the area you have spread with thinset tile cement, the next step is to lay in the front and side half-tiles to bring the surface out to the edging. When all the foot-square sheets or 4" tiles are arranged evenly with a good, flat top surface, mix more of the cement, spread it on, and repeat the tile laying procedure until the whole area of the countertop has been tiled.

Next, a slightly stiffer batch of cement can be mixed to affix the outside corner edging tile to the edges of the counter, spacing out these molding pieces about 1/8" apart. Soak the corner molding pieces in water before buttering each one on the inside surface prior to setting in place. When each tile has been laid, align it with the previous tiles set, with the help of a straightedge. When you reach the end of one side of edging, you'll probably find that the last remaining space to be covered with a molding piece is too short for the tile. When this happens, leave the space blank for the time being and start on the next side to be edged.

You can cut the last tile pieces on each edge before setting any of the tiles by placing them in position without cement and then marking the cut line for the last tile in the row. But then, if any slight variation creeps into your spacing of the tiles when you actually lay them, the cut piece will no longer fit. This is why we like to cut the last tiles after the others are actually in place.

The round, wirelike diamond chip saw blades that fit into hacksaw frames make short work of cutting through tile edging pieces. When you've marked and cut all the end pieces on each side edging of the countertop, you can put in the edging around the lip of the sink in the same way—lay a corner piece, then lay the pieces down one side until you can't fit another whole piece in; lay the next corner piece and then set the following pieces down the side, and so on, working all the way around the sink.

When all the tiles are in place over the whole counter area, let the job sit for a day to dry out before the grout is put in between the tiles.

Grouting

The grouting is a rather enjoyable job that makes all your tiling efforts suddenly look attractive—or should we say, even more attractive.

It comes in a variety of colors, and if you get fussy, you can even mix up a special color to suit your particular tile. When you have the shade you think will enrich the color of the tile, mix it up a little thinner than the tilesetting cement and with a sponge lightly wet down the area to be grouted. Then dig in, smearing the grout in circles and back and forth to work it into the cracks between the tiles and to work out all the air bubbles. Wipe the tile face of the grouted area reasonably clean and move on to the next area to be grouted. Grout between all the tiles over the entire surface and then in the capping molding along the edges and around the sink.

By this time the first area grouted will usually be set enough to start cleaning up. With a dampened sponge clean the tile of grout and smooth the grout between the tiles at the same time. Dip the sponge in water to clean it off every so often.

When all the grout is smoothed to the same level between all the tiles, and all the globs of grout have been removed from the face of the tiles, let the job sit for a couple of hours. When the grout has set up hard, you can start to clean off the face of the tiles once more with the sponge. After all the tile is clean, all the grout is in, and all the spills are wiped off the floor, you can let the counter sit overnight; then spray it with a protective silicone coating to keep the grout from becoming stained. One spraying lasts for about six months, so repeat the process a couple of times a year to make the counter easier to wipe clean no matter what spills on it.

Laying Tile on a New Surface and in Shower Enclosures

If you're planning to lay tile where there was once a different counter material, or on a new surface, the job is carried out in much the same way with a somewhat more involved preparation. There are really two ways of laying new tile on a surface such as a countertop. One is a rather involved method of building a 1-1/2" deep box over the counter area so that expanded iron wire mesh can be laid down. Then a thick layer of tile set base cement is mixed and poured into the area and screeded flat. When the cement is set, you have the same sort of base to work with that you find when you replace old tile.

The easier way to get the tile down is to build a flat, solid base out of 3/4" or 1" thick plywood (exterior grade). Then the tile, or tile sheets, can be fixed in place with a special tile adhesive which is spread on with a special serrated trowel. Once the adhesive has set the tiles firmly in place overnight, regular tile grout can be spread into the cracks between the tiles as in the more traditional process.

This adhesive is much easier to work with than the thinset tile cement because it gives you about an hour's worth of working time to get all the minor adjustments just right, compared to about ten minutes with the cement. The adhesive also permits an easy laying job when building tiled shower enclosures. A simple plywood (or special tile-backing wallboard) enclosure can be built (as shown in the illustrations) over a shower base pan. Then the adhesive can be spread on a few square feet at a time, working from the top down, and the tiles, or sheets of tiles, can be laid into the adhesive in a leisurely way and adjusted for squareness. The next day the grouting can commence, and on the third day the shower can be used.

Because tile adhesive is so easy to manage, one is sometimes tempted (when faced with the problem at all) to spread the stuff over an existing tile surface to lay a new surface of tiles. Although we've heard of such goings-on, we've also heard that the tile and the grout both tend to work loose under heavy use when laid in this way, so it seems to be a technique to be avoided.

Laminated Plastic Veneer

The other of the two most popular counter surfaces is that plastic veneer stuff that lovers of the real and the authentic despise so much. We must admit, that although laminated plastic veneer has its place, in large doses it can turn a perfectly innocent kitchen into a roadside diner. Not only that, it's not really as practical as one would like to believe. It's not above getting pretty well scratched over the years, and such counters are famous for having to have large amounts of square footage replaced just to fix one burned spot. Which reminds us—it *does* scorch without too much objection.

But then again, it's very popular, so we suppose some discussion will ensue on how to avail yourself of it at a minimum expense.

The Steps Involved in Laying Laminated Plastic Veneer

For small counters and around a bathroom sink (as in the bathroom pullman counter project), the veneer is fairly easy to work with. Mark on the front face of the sheet the outline to be cut to fit the material over the counter area and then run masking tape over these marks and redraw the lines.

Because the surface tends to flake up along the cut, try to use a continuous-motion saw such as a bandsaw or even an electric circular saw (rather than a reciprocating blade saw such as a saber or jig saw). If a hand-held circular saw is used, mark the dimensions on the back of the sheet.

The greatest difficulty for an amateur in working with this material is cutting it and, as a consequence, edging it. So before you plan to use it in a project, it may be well to figure a way to hide the cuts under moldings and edgings if you're new to working with the material.

Even if you're a seasoned old hand, it's hard to get a really professional edging to the stuff. It takes both special tools and techniques to get a "pro" appearance. Laying it with the special contact cement also has its scary moments. The adhesive is allowed to dry slightly before joining the parts, and once in place (or rather, once stuck together, whether in place or not), the sheet almost instantly becomes nearly impossible to adjust if the position isn't quite perfect.

So after slathering on the glue and letting it get tacky, as instructed, align one edge of the sheet in perfect position before allowing the sheet to lie down on top of the glue on the counter base.

As we said, most amateur builders can handle small areas to be covered with the veneer—especially if the material is covered with a countertop mounted sink and then trimmed with moldings. But if the counter is a large one stretching out both ways from the sink for any distance; if there is to be a long, exposed edging; and if the sink is mounted to the bottom of the counter surface, then it's best to get a professional in on the job.

If this is the choice and you'd still like to keep the expense down to a minimum, then you can do much of the preparatory work yourself before the pro is called in. There are several ways to handle the situation. You can build up a removable countertop of plywood and then take it into the shop to be covered with the plastic. Or you can cover the counter in place with a plywood base for the counter surface and then call in a pro to cover it. Or you can forget the whole thing and let a professional cabinetmaker handle the job from start to finish. To pay cabinetmakers' wages just to remove the old surface and build a new plywood base is, perhaps, not the cleverest move economically.

On the other hand there are certain transportation, measurement and installation problems involved in having the counter finished at the shop. There are all sorts of little mounting and joining problems that crop up when you build something in one place and install it in another. So we think the best compromise is to do the ripping out of the old and the mounting in place of the new counter base yourself. Then call in those with the special tools and know-how to give the counter a professionally finished look—for a professionally finished straight-edge look is just about the main attraction of this material; without it, there's not much to make it appealing.

Building a Base for Laminated Plastic Veneer

What is needed for a base is a firm, flat surface with very smooth edge cuts. Cut a sheet of 3/4" or 1" thick exterior plywood to fit over the area. Then nail battens ripped from 1" stock around the bottom of the sheet with their outside edges perfectly flush with the smooth, straight edges of the plywood to provide an exposed edging surface thicker than the plywood itself. Since the manufacturers of plywood do a good job of cutting straight edges, try to incorporate as many factory-cut edges of the sheet into the counter edging as possible.

Cut out the outline around the sink as smoothly as possible, and then sand off any remaining irregularities—if the sink is mounted to the bottom of the counter surface. With top-mounted sinks with a flange sitting down on the surface, or with flush-mounted stainless steel sinks using a mounting ring, this cut does not have to be quite so exact.

Next cut a 1" x 3" splashboard to fit on top of the counter, back up against the wall; nail it in place. If there is old wall mounted tile to be covered, cut a sheet of plywood to fit over this area, high enough to include a batten cut from 1" stock to be mounted to the back of the sheet, flush with the top edge (as on the counter surface base edges).

If the old counter is tile-covered, you may be able to mount the new base right over the old surface—*if* the sink can be brought up to meet the new countertop level. This process usually involves taking out the old sink and examining the mounts (usually a simple batten arrangement nailed to the surrounding cabinetry, or clamps mounted to the underside of the surface). If a new sink is to be installed anyway, this may make things even simpler.

To mount the plywood firmly down onto the top of the old tile, remove all tile edgings and anything else that would hold the new base up off the old surface. Then take out the old sink and either remount it higher by the thickness of the new base or make arrangements to mount a new sink on the new plywood surface. Next drill 1/4" holes down through the plywood, spaced out about one foot apart over the top of the counter base. With the new base in position, mark the exact positions of these holes in the base onto the top of the old tile.

Remove the new base and with a centerpunch make a small dent in the old tile surface exactly at each hole mark. With a 1/4" masonry bit for the electric drill, drill down through the tile at each of these points and insert a 1/4" plastic screw anchor and tap one down into each hole with a hammer.

Place the counter back into position with the sink in the proper spot and inset all screw holes so that the heads of the screws will not stick up above the surface of the base. Fasten the base down in position by sinking 2" number 8 or number 10 flathead wood screws down into the plastic anchors. Now you're all set to have the new surface covered with veneer.

Linoleum Countertops

Linoleum sheeting can make a surprisingly lasting countertop surface and is reasonably easy to work with if the areas aren't too large. Build much the same sort of base used for the plastic surface (without the battens around the edges) and attach the base in the same way to the cabinetry. Then cut the linoleum to the exact shape, using a framing square and a linoleum knife. Allow a little overlapping at the front edge (make use of the straight edge already cut on the sheeting to form the back edge). Linoleum can't be bent over the right-angle edge at the front, but you *can* bend it with a reasonably short-radius inside curve to run the surface sheeting vertically up the splashboard at the back of the counter. To do this, allow for the width of the splashboard on the back of the linoleum before cutting. Then just prior to laying the sheet, warm the linoleum over a heater or in the sun to get it a little more pliable. Next place the sheet face down over the edge of a table or bench and work back and forth over the length of the bend line to curve the sheeting into as tight a corner as you can without cracking the material.

Spread the linoleum adhesive all over the surface to be covered, using a special serrated trowel made for the purpose. Then stick the material in place, starting along the top edge of the splashboard and then firmly smoothing the material down onto the surface of the counter. Trim off the excess at the front edge with the linoleum knife. Run moldings along the front edges and top of the splashboard edge. A good, long-lasting variety for this purpose is a vinyl-covered wood molding with imitation wood grain. Because it's really wood inside, it's easy to cut and nail. And because it's imitation wood on the outside, it's easy to keep clean, doesn't stain and comes prefinished to your liking.

18

Miscellaneous Built-In Projects: Shelves, Shadowboxes, Doors and Hanging Tables

Shelves

Occasional shelves, or simple, exposed wall shelves, can be used throughout the house to add function and interest to blank bits of wall space. As these contrast with the surrounding wall texture by nature, they look better in rough-hewn, antiqued wood textures than in modern motifs which lend themselves to more integrated basic lines.

Much of the visual interest in old-style occasional shelves lies in the supporting corbels bracing up the shelf from beneath rather than in the actual shelf itself. The most common mistake is made not in the shape of the corbel but rather in its proportions. So it's important to get the basic proportions right. They are supposed to be made of sturdy stuff, from hewn logs and timbers and the like; nothing looks quite so self-defeating as a large corbel profile brace made from thin wood stock. The two straight edges of a corbel made from 1" stock cannot exceed about 4" without beginning to look thin and skimpy. A 2" stock corbel can go up to about 6", and corbels from this size up to about 8" on either side should be made from 4" thick stock. Since what you need to make corbels are short lengths of wide, thick lumber, you can often find just what you're looking for around the cut-off saws at the local lumberyard. If they don't let you have the cut-off scraps free, the charge will be very minor—and a great deal less than having to buy a whole board which usually comes in six-foot minimum lengths.

To get what you need, don't ask the attendants whether they have any scraps so big; find them yourself and then ask how much they want for the few measly pieces of wood. That way you won't be wasting their time, and they'll usually show their appreciation.

One way to mount such a shelf is to draw a horizontal line using the level at the height and placement desired. If the mounting is on an existing cabinet, then screw holes can be drilled through the backing and screws can be driven through into the back edge of the shelf.

The corbels can then be attached to the shelf by drilling screw holes down through the shelf, and then drilling countersink holes down into these with a

3/8" drill bit, halfway through the shelf board. After the corbels have been screwed in place, the holes can be filled with sort plugs cut from 3/8" dowels.

If the shelf is to be mounted on a flat wall surface, either you can find the positions of the studs along the horizontal positioning line in the wall and drive long nails angled down through the back edge of the shelf into the studs; or a 1" x 1" cleat can be nailed into the studs just below the positioning line, and then the shelf with corbels can be nailed down onto this cleat.

Corbeled Shelf

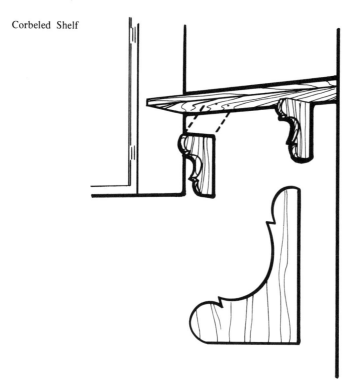

Shadowboxes

To build a shadowbox into the normal sort of hollow-core wall, we first have to make darned sure where we want the thing, for once you start making a shadowbox, there's no going back unless you panel over the whole area with a new surface.

To do this, cut out the outline of the proposed shadowbox from colored paper or cardboard. For most purposes, a small shadowbox, fitting between two of the wall studs, will do the job admirably without weakening the structure of the wall. Since we're dealing with the hard, straight lines of the boxlike rooms in most houses, the shadowbox is a good excuse to work in a curved line, arched over the top. This can either take the form of a Mediterranean style arch or be carried out with an arched beam, made up from a composite of boards in a simple fashion, as shown in the illustrations. The arched beam has a gentler curve and sticks out to either side of the end walls of the shadowbox, creating a very authentic built-in appearance.

When you have a general idea of the location, find the studs in the wall and draw the horizontal base line with the help of a level between these studs. (In case you missed the stud-finding technique mentioned in other projects, tap lightly on the wall with a hammer to locate spots where the wall seems to sound a little less hollow than usual. The studs are placed with their centers 16" apart, so start working along the line in the other direction about 15" away until you run up against the next stud.)

Draw the outline of the shadowbox in position on the wall, and then start knocking out the wallboard material from the center of the area outward toward the studs. Chip away a little at a time with the hammer and chisel toward the edges. If cutting out an arch form, use a piece of cardboard as a pattern to get a symmetrical shape. Fold it in half, cut it to the shape of a half arch and then unfold it. For shadowboxes with a slightly arched beam at the top, cut the surfacing away straight across the top, 3-1/2" above the bottom position of the beam.

Cut two short lengths of 2" x 4" and nail one of them to the side of each stud, forming the side walls of the shadowbox, so that the top ends of the 2" x 4"s are flush with the bottom of the shadowbox opening. Cut out the base shelf about 4" longer than the width of the distance between the side walls of the box. Cut the shelf piece so that it will fit back into the opening between the studs yet stick out to both sides in front of the wall. The depth of the shelf can be any dimension, of course; but if the overall depth is to exceed 8", then corbels should be included under the shelf for the sake of design.

The end corners facing outward from the wall can be rounded off or shaped with concave circular cuts for added visual interest. The shelf piece can be nailed down on the top ends of the short lengths of 2" x 4" attached to the sides of the studs.

Cut a 30" x 3-1/2" piece of expanded iron plaster backing (available at most yards); stuff it up into the space above the box so that it curves over about one inch above the curve of the arch; nail it to the sides of the mesh to the studs above the point where the arch comes tangent to the sides of the studs.

Mask off the shelf below with tape and newspaper, and then prepare a batch of plaster mix found in sacks at lumberyards (not patching plaster or plaster of Paris). Smear on a reasonably smooth surface to the bottom side of the arch, blending in the surface with the existing wall. While you're at it, fill in the vertical cracks where the studs meet the back of the wallboard in the back corner of the box. Then sand, stain or varnish the shelf and corbels, and paint the box to match the wall. Painting it the same color as the wall will give you all the interest you need to break up the wall without making the box look like an afterthought—which it is, of course. Painting the box a contrasting color results in a harsh, overdramatic look in our opinion; but it's your house.

To make the arched beam, cut a length of 4" x 4" stock to fit horizontally between the two studs. Mark the outline of the beam on a length of 1" x 8" or 1" x 10" stock, extending out 2" beyond the width of the box on both sides.

Wall Component

Cut out this shape with a coping saw, saber saw or bandsaw; and then place the beam front piece in position, leveled at the top of the shadowbox. Draw the outline of the beam onto the wall, and then cut away the wall covering around this outline, using a hammer and chisel and keeping the cut as close to the outline as possible. Nail the beam centered over the 4" x 4", flush at the bottom edge. Next cut the 4" x 4" so that it follows the bottom curve of the beam, giving an authentic look of depth to the beam. Place the beam assembly, with the 4" x 4" attached, in the hole cut for it in the wall and nail the front piece of the beam to the two studs against which the ends of the beam front sit.

Shadowbox

Spackling paste or a bit of plaster mix or patching plaster can be used to fill in the cracks around the edge of the beam, and the corner cracks between the side wall studs and the wallboard backing, before the painting and staining commence.

How To "Distress" Wood

With all occasional shelves, "beams," and decorative antique cornice boards which are stained or varnished, you may want to give a hand-hewn look to the edgings and what is known as a "distressed" (or beat-up) look to the surfaces. This not only lends an attractive air of authenticity to shelves with an antique theme but also covers up a host of minor mistakes.

To give a hand-hewn look to the corner edges, run a serrated drum-rasp attachment for an electric drill along the edgings, rounding off the corners and giving a slightly irregular feel to the corners. Then go over the wood with a medium-fine grade of sandpaper to smooth down the surface without removing the random irregularities.

The standard old joke about distressing wood surfaces is the one that has to do with loading your shotgun with light birdshot and then simply standing back and blasting away at the project (before mounting it in place, preferably). We must confess we've never tried that one.

However, we have managed to come up with a few methods of our own for removing the obvious "newness" of a wood surface, and giving it the rich texture of age, that sound just about as strange as the birdshot technique.

One way to give a randomly distressed look (and it has to be random to avoid looking contrived) is to find a walkway or driveway covered with pea gravel. Place the project to be distressed face down in the gravel and jump on it until the proper effect is achieved. This not only makes a marvelous surface when stained and wiped lightly but also gives one a strange feeling of satisfaction in the process.

You can also allow the kids of the neighborhood to use the piece in question as a target for a bit of rock-throwing practice. Then the corners and edges can be tapped lightly and evenly with a hammer to remove any remaining sharp corners. No matter how battered the piece may look after either of these brands of punishment, once it has been wiped with stain to deepen the irregularities, it will have a rich, seasoned look when mounted in place.

Doors

Paneled doors will fit into a wide variety of room styles and can be made reasonably easily if you happen to have access to a table saw. The basic idea is to take an old door (the type with a thick framework surrounding a center panel of thinner wood) and cover it with the panels cut on the table saw. After you've found an inexpensive door that looks ripe for paneling (try the local secondhand lumberyard), lay out the arrangement of panels evenly on the door itself with a pencil and a framing square. Then cut the panel pieces and the divider frames from 1" stock with an attractive grain pattern if stain or varnish is to be used.

Next set the saw blade so that it cuts a kerf only about 1/4" to 3/8" deep, and set the rip guide so that you can make a cut this deep and 2" in from the edge of the board as it is passed through the saw. Cut each panel on all four sides so that there are four grooves cut across each other on the face of the panel.

Paneled Door

Set the saw blade so that it will make a 2" deep cut, then tilt the blade at about five degrees and set the rip guide about 1/4" or 3/8" away from the base of the blade so that it will slice a 1/4" or 3/8" wedge off the edge of the panels and 1/4" at the grooves. Running each panel through on edge, slice away the beveled border around the center of each panel, cutting all four edges of each panel.

Attach the panels and the panel separators to the door with brads or finishing nails and white glue. You can then use a wood rasp or a serrated shaper drum attachment for the electric drill to bevel off the edges of the panel separators, starting and ending the beveling about an inch from the end of each exposed edge.

The outboard ends of the panel separators can be beveled down to meet the existing frame around the door, or you can look around for 1/4" or 3/8" thick lumber stock to cut to size and nail down over the framing of the door, with the boards in the same position as the existing frame boards.

The Hanging Table

The hanging table is a built-in project that is guaranteed to excite comment. The project itself may be a little involved in places for the beginning builder, but the overall cost is a fraction of the price of a large dining table. So, if you're in the market for new dining furniture, you may want to look into the possibilities of adapting such a table to your own use. Although it seems to get a predictably good reaction from all who see the table it isn't everyone who wants to invest time and effort in such out-of-the-ordinary projects. However, for the more daring builders in the crowd, here are the general rules for building hanging tables.

Construction of the Table

Hanging tables are nothing new on the scene; every so often a current variety is seen creating an exciting, innovative setting on a two-page spread in a shelter magazine. There's one way to find out whether the designer of the project pictured has ever actually lived with a hanging table or not: If the table is attached very solidly to mother earth in two places at one end, the table will work. If it isn't, the table will be so unsteady that it will be useless for most practical purposes.

Hanging tables with one end or one side attached to a nearby wall will work out nicely. Even though the one pictured in the illustration seems to be supported by some antigravity device, it's actually held up in position on one end with a hefty 1/4" iron box section brace. So you can see that you need more than suspension chains to keep this type of table from spilling the wine in your lap every time someone tries to cut a tough steak.

To build this example, the first step is to make the bench seat which rounds the corner of the room and runs under one end of the table. Horizontal cleats or spacers made from 2" x 12" stock are securely fastened to the walls at a level about three inches below the level of the corner seat (with the top edges at about 12"). The seating, as well as the table itself, is made from two layers of clear 2" x 12" stock, with the lumber running in different directions in both layers.

The boards of the bottom layer are cut to angle across one way, with the ends cut exactly to fit up against the wall, and the other ends cut off a little beyond the contour of the front edge of the seat bench. The contour is drawn on the boards, and then the hand-held circular saw is used to score about a

Another moneysaving project for the more ambitious builder is a hanging dining table. Although the actual construction is simple, hefty engineering is involved to anchor the table securely to mother earth so that the peas won't fall in your lap every time someone cuts a steak. Beware the hanging table project that isn't to the earth secured.

Miscellaneous Built-In Projects

Hanging Table

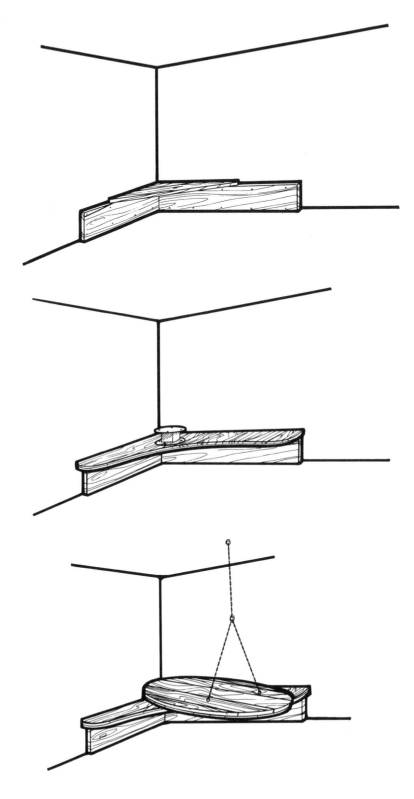

3/8" deep groove along this line. Then the cut of the blade is adjusted to make a cut about 3/8" deeper, and another pass is made with the saw over the same groove. This process is repeated several times, increasing the depth of the blade cut every time until the unwanted wood has been cut away.

Then the second layer is nailed onto the top of the bottom layer with finishing nails, and the front edge contour is cut in the same manner. Once the bench seat is built, you can build the iron support in a number of ways. You can cut the curved pieces shown in the photos to make a graceful support; but because the brace is very rarely seen, you may want to make a simpler brace by cutting four pieces of 1/4" thick iron measuring 8" x 12", along with two pieces 12" x 12". The four pieces are welded together along the 12" edge to form a 12" long square tube, 8" on a side. Then the ends of the tube are welded centered to the 12" x 12" pieces, one on either end. A 3/8" hole is drilled through all eight corners of the two 12" x 12" pieces, about 1" in from the sides.

Place this fabrication directly under the proposed position of the tabletop, drill 1/4" starter holes into the wood through the 3/8" holes in the iron and then attach the weldment to the top of the bench with 2" x 3/8" lag bolts extending down through the bottom flange of the weldment and into the top of the bench.

The longitudinal top layer boards are cut to approximate length and are laid out in position, face down, on a flat surface. Then the cross boards are cut to approximate length and nailed and glued down onto the top of the table after it has been flipped over, and the boards are trimmed (with straight cuts) to within 1" of the contour.

The final contouring is done with repeated passes of the power saw, making a slightly deeper cut with each pass. In this way even quite thick stock can be cut in a fairly tight outside curve. Inside curves cannot be cut quite as tightly because the trailing edge of the blade tends to ruin the edge that you want to keep. Trim away excess under the path of the cut with a handsaw which will follow the groove made by the power saw.

Hanging the Table

When the tabletop has been cut, drill two 1/2" or 5/8" holes in it, as shown, equidistant from the centerline, and insert two 1/2" or 5/8" eyebolts through the table; secure them with washers and nuts. Separate chains or two chains running to a single hanging chain can be run up and secured to a rafter or ceiling joist. If the joists are hidden above a drywall ceiling, the chains can run up through a hole in the ceiling and into a hefty 5/8" eyebolt extending horizontally through a rafter, about 2" down from its top edge.

Block the table up level and attach the chains; run lag bolts up through the holes in the top flange of the weldment and into the bottom of the tabletop. Then remove the supports. Round off all corner edges with a serrated shaper and sand the table and bench smooth. Finish to your taste. The table pictured was simply oiled after sanding.

19

Windows, Mirrors and Tub Enclosures

Although this isn't a maintenance book in the truest sense, and we're more concerned with improving than with keeping up, there are times in fitting antique windows or French doors into a house that you'll find yourself needing a pane or two of glass replaced. So we'll cover the processes involved just to be on the safe side.

Preparation for Repairing Broken Windows

Place newspaper on the floor beneath the window in question and very carefully (using a rag to cover the glass where necessary) pry the broken bits of glass loose from the mounting putty. A firm but slow and steady push to one side and then the other will usually loosen up the glass and allow it to be pulled free. When all but the smallest, most stubborn pieces have been removed, use a hammer and sharp wood chisel to chip away all the old putty surrounding the pane.

Remove all remaining glazing points left in the wood frame and clean the area around the pane. Measure the height and width of the frame. Then mark and cut a piece of glass 1/8" shorter and 1/8" narrower than these measurements. In most cases (where you don't usually have suitable scraps of glass lying around ready to be cut), simply phone the exact measurements (indicating that you have already reduced the overall dimensions by 1/8") to the local glass supplier. He can cut you a piece simply and cheaply from his stock of scraps, and you can pick it up for installation a little later in the day.

For areas to be glazed up to about 18" square, double-strength (1/8" thick) glass will usually do the job. For areas up to about three feet square, crystal (3/16") will do, and for larger areas use plate glass (1/4" thick). Plate glass is also usually a good deal flatter than crystal, so if you're interested in looking at a nice, undistorted view through the window, use plate.

Cutting Glass and Mirrors

Cutting techniques vary a little from thickness to thickness. Generally, the thicker the glass, the easier it is to cut. However, even thick textured glass is hard for a beginner to cut because the break will want to follow the texture lines more than the scored line. If you do attempt to cut textured glass always score it on the smooth side.

The general procedure for cutting glass is the same used for cutting mirrors. The more you learn about glass, the less you take it for granted. It is a supercooled liquid, not a solid, and it can react in very strange ways. It's very flexible (up to a point, and a real pro knows just where this point is); it's even elastic (a glass ball dropped on a hard surface will bounce higher than a rubber ball—if it doesn't shatter first); and the experts tell us that it's softer on the inside than it is on the surface. Herein lies the secret of how it can be cut by scratching it along a line.

The basic idea is to break up this surface along the line, and then put this surface in tension by placing the sheet over a fulcrum just under this line. The only trouble is, as soon as a line is scored, it begins to "cool off" or "heal," which makes it no longer the path of least resistance for a break. So you have to move reasonably fast after the scoring line has been cut. Not only that, if you press too hard on the cutter when you score the line, the cut will be too "hot" and little chips will pop out of the cut, presenting opportunities for the break to wander away from the line at every chip.

So the only real secret to be practiced is getting just the right amount of pressure on the cutter. For this purpose you round up some glass scraps of the same thickness as the piece to be cut (for pressure will vary according to the thickness) and a little practice should take place. The scoring should be made in one, reasonably firm, steady swipe of the cutter. If you have to go back over the scoring to fill in some missed spots, you're courting disaster.

The cutting method also depends on the position of the cut on the panel of glass. If the cut is to run within 1/2" of the existing edge, the notches in the side of the cutter are used to grip the edge of the glass near one end of the cut, and then pressure is applied in a firm, snapping motion to break the trim piece down and away from the pane. If the cut comes within 3" of the existing edge of the glass, the back side of the pane is tapped with the ball at the end of the cutter handle to start the break. Then pliers are positioned just to the outside of the end of the break line and the glass is given a gentle twisting from the end to peel the trim strip away from the cut line.

If the cut comes within 6" of an existing edge, the glass is placed on a firm, padded surface with the score line facing upward along the edge of the surface (such as a towel over a tabletop). Starting at one end of the cut, the overhanging trim part is given a gentle slapping, down and away from the score line.

For cuts farther away from the edge of the glass sheet, a slat about 1/4" thick (like a yardstick) is slipped under the sheet just after the scoring is made, and positioned parallel to the break line, about 1/4" in toward the portion of glass to be kept. Then, starting at the edge of the glass closest to you, place the palms of both hands down on the glass about eight inches to both sides of the cut and give a firm, downward push. If the break doesn't continue all the way across of its own volition give another downward push farther along to help it across.

To do the scoring: After the positions of the cuts have been marked on the glass, start with the shorter cuts, reducing the length of the longer cuts made later. Place the sheet down on a firm, flat, padded surface and have someone help hold a 1/4" x 2" batten about 1/8" to the left side of the mark (if you're right-handed).

Paint the area along the mark with a thin coat of motor oil to keep the cut "cool," run the cutter very lightly over the cut line once or twice to loosen up the wheel and get some oil on it. Then, starting at the end away from you (holding the cutter like a pen), draw the cutter toward you firmly and without letting it slow down too much. It seems to be more important to keep the pressure steady than to get exactly the right amount of push. Make sure you've mapped out just what you want to do after the scoring line is cut, and have all the tools within easy reach. Then break the glass without spending any time having to stand around and think about it.

Mounting Glass

To mount a pane of glass, first knead a handful of glazier's putty for a few minutes to warm it up and make it more pliable. Place a wad of the putty in your palm and then force it into the border around the opening that the glass will cover. Work the putty along, using more as you need it to leave about a 1/2" beading around the frame.

Push the pane of glass into place around the edges to smooth out the putty so that between the front of the glass and the frame there is about 1/8" to 1/4" of putty sandwiched in to make a leakproof seal.

Glazier's "push-points" (little metal prongs that can be pushed into the wooden framing to hold the glass in place) are the easiest fasteners to work with. Simply push them into place against the back of the glass with a screwdriver. Lacking these, you can use small brads or finishing nails to hold the glass securely. The brads should be nailed into the framing, positioned up against the back of the glass. Make sure the nails are not so long that they will poke through the frame and crack the adjoining pane of glass.

To drive in nails next to glass, place the side of the hammer *firmly* against the pane of glass and slide it up and down while still in contact with the glass at the side, driving the nail down, leaving about 3/8" of it showing. If you try to hold the hammer away from the glass it will eventually hit it and crack the new pane, no matter how careful you are. So let the side of the hammer slide on the glass as you pound.

Force more putty around the edge frame of the pane and then use the end of a putty knife to remove the excess and to force the putty firmly into the cracks, making a beveled border around the glass.

Installing Mirrors

The simplest and often most effective way to wall-mount mirrors is to use

187

what is commonly referred to as a "J-bar" and plastic clips. This "J-bar" is a J-shaped aluminum extrusion, available at glass and paint stores, which remains, for the most part, hidden once the mirror is in place. If you're mounting on a plaster or wallboard wall, first find the vertical positions of the studs, which are centered 16" apart in the wall behind the mirror area. Draw a light pencil line along the top of a level to mark the bottom of the mirror. Now cut the "J-bar" 1/8" shorter than the length of the bottom side of the mirror and file the ends smooth. Place the "J-bar" with its bottom along the mounting line and drive in small box nails through the back of the bar and into the studs at two or more points. Make certain that the nailheads don't stick out where they can scratch the back of the mirror, and check the levelness of the bar mounting. Now place two small 1/8" x 3/4" strips of soft lead or wood about 1/16" thick in the trough of the bar, about 3" in from the end. If you're mounting a very large mirror, use more strips, about two feet apart. Then place two or three small bits of thick rubber tape on the wall near the upper corners of the mirror for padding. Next place a plastic mirror clip and a nail somewhere handy and slip the bottom edge of the mirror down the wall and into the "J-bar." Insert the nail through the hole in the clip and mark the position of the clip hole when the clip is in place against the top edge of the mirror, making two marks at equal distances from the top corners of the mirror. Take the mirror down by lifting up and then pulling it away from the wall. Make starter holes for the clip mounting screws at the marks with a hammer and a nail. Then place the clips, screws and a screwdriver where they can easily be reached. Replace the mirror carefully, avoiding any scratches on the backside, and then screw the clips in place.

The soft lead allows the mirror glass to "creep" as it expands and contracts with changes in temperature without binding up and cracking. Metal clips can also be used to mount mirrors, especially the three-panel, swing-out makeup type table mirrors. To mount these, mark the outline of the mirror on the wall, making sure it's level before marking. Then nail on the clips, spaced evenly around the mirror outline with the mounting surface of the "J-bar" clips aligned with the mirror outline. Plastic clips can be used in this way by themselves without the "J-bar," at least for smaller mirrors.

Glass Tub Enclosures

You can save money by buying a tub enclosure assembled in a local shop and installing it yourself. There's rarely an instruction book for putting it in, however, so here is the general process.

Tub enclosures, whether they be sliding glass, pivoting glass, plastic or even flexible plastic, are all mounted in pretty much the same sort of frame. They're almost always made of extruded aluminum, with the top piece carrying the sliding track, the bottom serving as a guide and water gutter and the sides holding the top and bottom members in place. The vertical side pieces are generally precut to the proper length, but the top and bottom pieces have to be specifically fitted to each set of walls surrounding the tub (for, although this may come as a shock to some, very few walls are actually straight).

Installing the Frame

The first thing to do is measure the distance along the top of the tub on the near side, between the walls. Measure this exactly, taking into consideration the measuring tape case, and so on, and then subtract 3/8". Cut the bottom piece to this resulting length as squarely as possible, using a hacksaw. The bottom member is the one with the two troughs in it, and the little drain holes to one side, in the sliding models.

Place the bottom piece on top of the tub's edge, holding it aligned as best you can to the center of the top of the tub side. Place the side pieces in position, one at a time, aligned vertically with the lay of the tiling. While the side pieces are in place, mark the position of the mounting holes on the tile (or waterproof wall covering). Remove the pieces and mark the mounting holes with a centerpunch, making a small dent in the tile. Now drill through the tile or wall covering at these points with a 1/4" masonry bit. Place 1/4" plastic screw anchor inserts in these holes with a hammer.

Place the bottom ends of the side pieces overlapping the ends of the bottom piece and sink the flathead screws into the holes to fix the side members in place. Run the middle screw of each side through a rubber bumper before screwing it in. If your bottom piece doesn't have a rubber sealer strip along the bottom, you may want to place a line of white vinyl tub caulking (which comes in a tube) along the bottom side of the bottom piece before placing it in position under the overlapping ends of the side pieces.

Once the sides and bottom are in place, measure exactly the distance between the side walls at the tops of the side pieces. Now cut the top piece to this length, file the ends smooth, and place it in position with its ends overlapping the top ends of the side pieces.

Installing the Panels

In the pivoted and flexible plastic editions, the hinging points of the panels will be attached as the top member is mounted. On the sliding panel types, the tracking wheels should be bolted onto the tops of the panels at this point. The smooth side of the glass should face the interior of the bath enclosure on both panels, with the panel nearest the shower head riding the inner track. Before mounting the panels, however, small plastic clip guides should be mounted on the bottom edges of the panels with screws. Then each panel in turn can be lifted up, smooth side in, into the troughs next to the tracks in the top member. By lifting the wheels up and over the lip of the track, the panel can be let down in position with the wheels on the track and the bottom edge in the right guide trough in the bottom piece.

Once both panels are on and sliding, check the alignment of their side edges against the side pieces, and then as compared to each other. If their side frames sit at varying angles to each other, or to the side pieces, so that they

189

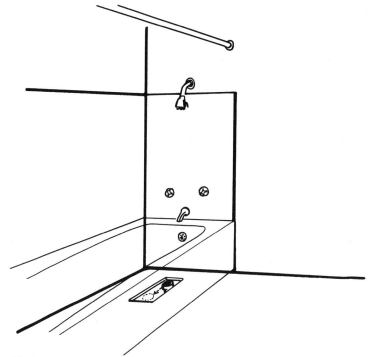

Shower Enclosure

can't close all the way at the top or bottom, remove the panel(s) and adjust the mounting of its wheels until it sits up closely at bottom and top against the sides. In extreme cases you'll have to strike a compromise between the angles of the various vertical members. Run a line of white vinyl tub caulking around the corner joints where the frame meets the tile or wall surface. To do this, snip off the end of the tube at an angle and squeeze a smooth, continuous narrow bead along the frame edge joints to seal in the water and improve appearances.

With the pivoting style, simply loosen the pivot pin mounting screws, hold the door in proper adjustment and tighten the mounting screws again.

20

Curtains and Cornice Boards

Whenever patterned material is to be brought into the field of view in a room, you have an opportunity to create really striking visual improvements in a single project (and you also have an opportunity to spend a good deal of the old hard-earned cash).

However, with a little quick thinking, it's usually possible to maximize the visual improvement while minimizing the financial drain. With curtains you have a number of courses at your disposal. You can call in the man from the drapery shop and have him figure out and put in what you need (but it will cost you dearly). You can figure what you need yourself, then look around for suitable stuff, ready-made, and save a good deal (however, you'll find the selection a little narrow). Or you can figure out what you need and then sew up the curtains yourself, using a great little laborsaver called "pleater tape," which allows the merest amateur to create truly professional-looking curtains.

By doing the sewing yourself, you'll suddenly find a host of new sources of imaginative materials opened up for you, giving you a much wider field of choice than with ready-made curtains. And you'll also find that the cost will be cut to a fraction.

There is still another variation of the do-it-yourself approach that can save even more. Often a room will have perfectly suitable but very dull curtains already in place. By adding colorful panels of material at both ends of the area to be curtained, you can get almost the same effect as all new curtains for a very nominal investment, thereby keeping the original curtains in service much longer but with a whole new look. Since the majority of curtains are open during the hours we view them anyway, the effect of the end-panel approach is very close to that of replacing the entire window area with new curtaining material.

Whatever your choice of alternatives turns out to be, we'll describe a typical installation job, using pleater tape, which makes the task literally within the capabilities of anyone. You can simply drop out the steps you'd rather have other people take care of, if that's your choice.

192

Curtains and Cornice Boards

Figuring the Job

The first task is to get an idea of how much material, pleater tape and hooks you'll need. Remember that the area to be covered is usually figured by the length of the curtain slide track or rod over the window. We'll cover the mounting of such a track later; but right now, the size of the curtains themselves will be figured.

To determine the vertical length of material needed, you first have to come to a decision about the general length of the curtains—should they be full length (from the curtain rod down to 1" above the floor); or should they be sill length (from the rod down to 1" below the sill frame beneath the window)?

Once this dilemma has been resolved, measure the distance from the curtain slide down to the level decided upon. If the top edge of the curtain is to extend up above the track to hide it slightly, add 1" to this measurement. Finally, add 6" to the total measurement (for the top and bottom hems) to get the correct length for each panel.

To figure the width needed to do the job, measure the length of the curtain slide (if a rod is used and it bends back at 90 degrees into the wall at the ends, then add the length of these short pieces to the total measurement).

Pleater tape uses specially fashioned wire clamp hooks to hold the material in attractive gathered pleats. When the material is so gathered, the width of the material is reduced by half; so simply double the length of the curtain slide or rod measurement. Then add 2" to this measurement for each panel of material needed to fill out the width; add another 2" for a split down the center if the curtain is to be drawn back on both sides of the window. This is the total width needed, as well as the length of pleater tape required, to curtain the window.

We'll measure the curtain material needed on a sample window just to make sure we haven't said everything backward.

For the sake of argument, let's say the window measures 54" across, and that you've decided full-length curtains will do the trick. We'll say that the slide is set 80" above the floor. Eighty inches, plus 1" to cover the track, minus 1" to clear the floor, plus 6" for the top and bottom hems comes out to 86", if our slide rule is working right. (The inch clearance at the bottom is to allow for a certain amount of stretch over the years, thanks to the force of gravity.)

If the track is 56" long (usually it's a bit wider than the window), then doubling that distance, we find we'll need about 112" of material, plus a little for hemming each panel. If we happen to be working with 48" wide material, then we'll need three panels. Adding 2" for hemming or seaming the side edges of each of the three panels, we come out with 112", plus 6", or 118" of width to be cut from the three panels. Add another 2" for the hems down the center cut, which splits the material into two equal curtains, and we come up with a total width of 120". If the curtain is to be gathered all on one side when open, the three panels can be seamed together. But if two curtains are to be

193

used, drawn back on each side of the window as is usually the case, then you'll want to use one full panel and one narrower panel, seamed together, on each side of the window.

To do this, we'll cut off three lengths of the material to the total vertical measurement (86"), and then a little simple arithmetic will show us how wide to cut the narrow panels. If the overall width of the material is to be 120", we'll need 60" of width for each of the two curtains for the window. To make each curtain, one panel will be 48" wide, and the other panel will be the remainder of the necessary measurement, or 12" in this case, to equal 60". With 1" taken up on both sides of each panel for end hems and a joining seam, the total width of each curtain when sewn together comes to 56"— which is the exact length of the curtain slide track (amazingly enough).

The leftover material from the narrow panel cuts can be used for covering cornice boards, matching pillows, tiebacks, and even covering the seats of dining room or bedroom chairs, and the like.

Always buy a little extra yardage when dealing with plaids and matching patterns so that the patterns on both curtains can be synchronized vertically. While you're shopping around for an inspiring material, make note of the practical side of the fabric as well—whether it's machine-washable, and so forth, which may make your decision a little easier.

Once again, the steps involved in supplying yourself with a new set of curtains in a room go something like this: make a rough sketch of the window(s) to be covered, noting down any peculiarities in the construction, or in the mounting of the curtain slide tracks, that might affect the curtaining; note also the dimensions of the window and the length of the slide track. Then take this sketch with you to a yardage shop and search through all sorts of fabrics—not only those that are traditionally associated with curtain use but all the other suitable materials that interest you. You may even want to check upholstery shops or linen displays to find a material that looks as if it would fire the creative spirit in you. Make note of the width of the material you like and then sit down somewhere quiet and figure out exactly what it will take to do your job.

For the sample we measured, we'll need three lengths of material 48" wide and 86" long. This comes to 21', 6" of the material, or seven yards and an extra 6". If you're cutting it close, you may be able to charm your way into getting the extra 6" for free. But if you can swing it, go ahead and round off the leftover to the next nearest yard, and you'll be sure to have enough for the job and maybe to cover a few matching room accessories.

When buying the pleater tape, you have a number of choices to make in order to get the right kind of tape and the right kind of hooks for your particular installation. First of all, the tape comes in both 3" and 4" widths—the narrower being used for sill length curtains. The hooks also come in 3" and 4" lengths to match, but there are other variations in the hooks. Some are made for hanging curtains to hide the slide track (with the hook halfway down the back of the pleater clamp), whereas others are made for use directly under ceilings or in slide tracks mounted on valance boards; still others are made for use with rings for café curtains. So buy enough of the proper width tape to cover the total width of the curtain material, and then pick up the type of hooks that will do the job for you.

In the usual sort of curtain, the hooks are spaced at 4" intervals, so simply divide the length of the tape in inches by four to get the number of hooks to buy, making sure you get two end hooks for each curtain.

Making the Curtains

When you get all the needed materials home, lay out the fabric on the floor and cut the necessary lengths (remember to leave enough over on each panel to align plaids or patterns, if necessary). Then cut the widths needed to make the narrow panels; sew these to the full-width panels with a 1" seam. Iron the seam open flat against the back of the material.

Next fold over the side edge of the curtain 1/2" and press flat against the back of the material. Then fold this flap over another 1/2" to make a double-folded hem. Pin this hem in place and then stitch.

To make the bottom hem, place the material backside-up on a flat surface and then fold along the bottom edge, pressing a 2-1/2" fold against the back

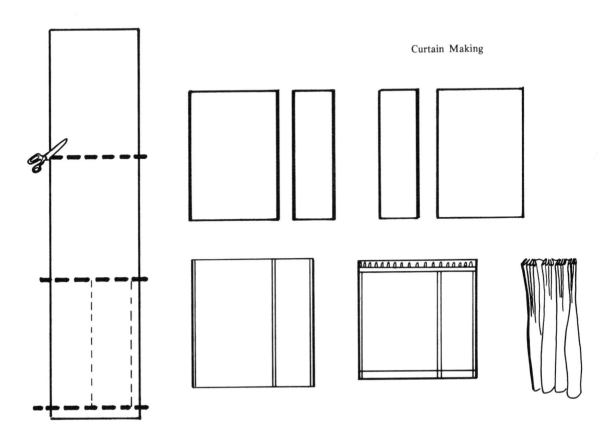

Curtain Making

of the material. Fold the material back another 2-1/2" and press it flat. Baste or pin the hem in place and then stitch. The bottom hem can be mitered at both ends if desired.

Attaching the Pleater Tape

To attach the pleater tape, turn back a 1" hem along the top edge of the curtain and press it flat against the back of the material. Cut the tape to the length of the top edge of the curtain. Place the curtain down, backside-up and then place the tape, *face up,* over the hem so that the top edge of the tape is 1/4" down from the top edge of the curtain. Make certain that the tape is right side up, with the open end of the pockets facing toward the *bottom* edge of the curtain. Fold the ends of the tape under a little and then pin or baste in place. Stitch around the guidelines printed on the tape, and then you're ready to install the pleater hooks.

Installing the Hooks

Beginning at one end of the curtain, place an end hook in the first pocket. Then skip a pocket and insert one of the four prongs on a pleater hook into each of the next four pockets, gathering the material so that the four pockets are bunched and the four prongs can all be pushed up into the adjoining pockets. Check the front side of the curtain to make sure all the gathered folds look even and then push the locking clip into place around the prongs.

Skip the next pocket, and then grab another hook and repeat the process with the following four pockets; move on down the tape until the whole curtain is pleated. And presto! There's a custom-made curtain using just the material you like and costing a fraction of the price of the dull, ready-made variety.

Hanging the Curtains

While we have curtains on the mind, we might as well describe how they're hung, in case you want to modify the existing setup or even make a new one.

Curtain hangers can be divided into two basic species: curtain rods and curtain slide tracks. The rods can be fluted wooden dowels, wrought iron bars with spearheads on the ends, simple metal rods bending back into the wall at 90 degrees on either end, and so forth. The slide tracks range from simple metal C-shaped slides, to be mounted against the bottom side of a valance board, all the way to ornate imitation fluted brass curtain rods with metal slides and a system of ropes and pulleys contained therein.

The fluted wooden dowels are simply mounted in metal or wooden brackets that can be screwed or nailed to the studs that run up both sides of the window behind the wall covering. The brackets should be mounted so that the dowel will sit horizontally, an inch or two above the window frame across the top, and positioned so that the screws will sink into the studs next to the side frames of the window.

Making Cornice Boards

A cornice board can be cut to the length of the dowel, plus 1-1/2". Then cut two short end pieces (usually about 3" long) to fit between the back of the cornice board and the wall. Assemble the cornice board with glue and 2" finishing nails, and then nail it in position (after staining, painting, or covering the board with material to match the decor of the room), using nails running in through the end boards and into the ends of the dowels.

To rig up a new curtain slide-cornice board combination, attach two 2" iron L-shaped braces, one on either side of the window. Position the braces so that one arm of the brace runs vertically down the wall just next to the side frames of the window, so that screws sunk through the holes in the L brace will bite into the studs on either side of the window. The other arm of the brace should extend out horizontally from the wall, 2" above the top window frame.

Cornice Boards

Cut a piece of 1" x 4" to the length of the proposed curtain width, and position this on top of the extended arm of the L brace, centered over the window. Then sink 3/4" screws through the holes in the brace and up into the bottom of the board. Cut off a length of the C-shaped curtain slide track to equal the length of the 1" x 4" and screw this track up onto the bottom of the 1" x 4", centered on the board.

Slip the necessary number of nylon glides into the end of the track itself, and rig up any pulley system you want to buy, to open the curtains with a pull of the cord (although these systems often turn out to be more trouble than they're worth). You can also slip the curtain hooks directly into the glides and use the old-fashioned pull-the-curtain-by-hand method, which saves you from getting all tangled up in fouled ropes and pulleys.

This apparatus can be covered by the cornice board by cutting a piece of 1" x 6" stock as long as the 1" x 4", plus 1-1/2". Cut two 3-1/2" lengths of 1" x 6" to be nailed behind the ends of the cornice as end boards; then paint, stain or cover the cornice and nail it to the exposed edges of the 1" x 4" already in place. Whenever planning cornice boards in this fashion, buy the type of pleater hook that allows the curtain to be hung down below the slide track.

21

Plumbing

As we've said several times before, the jobs explained in this book are primarily concerned with creating new features for the house rather than just presenting steps needed to maintain what's already there. The same is true with the plumbing section, but although the tasks involved are arranged to create new visual effects to replace the old, there's still plenty of material applicable to maintenance. If you hunt around through the related subjects, you can find a lot of projects that will help keep existing bathrooms in top shape.

Removing and Refitting Sink Taps and Drains

Start by turning off the water at the lead-in valves below the sink. If these valves show signs of leaking or deterioration, this may be a good opportunity to replace them also. To do this, shut off the water pressure for the entire house at the meter valve. Possibly there's a shut-off valve on the lead-in line as it enters the house. Even if you're not planning on getting deeper into the plumbing than the taps, it's always a good idea to track down the shut-off valve for the whole house when beginning any kind of plumbing repairs—just in case something embarrassing occurs somewhere along the line.

If you are planning to replace the lead-in valves, the process is this: turn on the taps to drain out any remaining head of water pressure. Loosen the fasteners holding the chrome inlet tubes which extend from the shut-off valves up to the bottoms of the taps, and remove the tubes from the valves; then pull the tubes down and out of the taps if the taps are to be replaced; otherwise, gently bend the tubes out of the way.

The most crucial point of any project dealing with old plumbing is where you remove the old fittings. The important thing here is not to allow any of the twist needed to remove the fitting to be transferred farther down along the line of pipes. The pipe on which the fitting-to-be-removed is mounted must be held firmly so that none of the twist can loosen a fitting farther down inside a wall where you can't get at it. So attach one wrench to the fitting and another, mounted in the opposite direction, to the pipe coming from the wall or floor;

then unscrew the fitting. If the threads are old and stubborn, try a light tapping on the wrench attached to the fitting. Make certain the wrench attached to the inlet pipe has a good grip before applying any real pressure to the other.

Once the old taps are off, wipe some pipe joint compound over the threads of the lead-in pipes and firmly attach the new shut-off valves, using the two wrenches in reversed positions.

The taps themselves come in varying mountings, depending usually on the vintage of the plumbing. Some old-style separate tap handles and spout (especially the wall-mounted variety) are difficult, if not impossible, to replace with new hardware that will fit the hole spacings. The most widely used mounting today accommodates the single unit tap and spout combination. A wide variety of different brands of taps-and-spout and even single handle taps can usually be mounted to this spacing of the three holes, centered about 2" apart. Faucets mounted in this fashion are held down against the top of the sink with washers and nuts running up from the bottom (on the same threads that hold the rubber washer fasteners which attach the water lead-in tubes to the bottoms of the taps). Remove these fasteners with a crescent or small monkey wrench, and then take off the retaining nuts which hold the unit to the sink. For tight corners, and especially if you're planning on making one or two counter cabinets, it may be wise to invest in an inexpensive tap-removal wrench which can loosen or tighten with a minimum of problems these mounting nuts way up under a counter. With sinks using a top-mounted stopper control, loosen the small set screw or bolt which fixes the vertical arm of the stopper pull to the lever coming out of the back of the drainpipe. Now the tap spout unit should come free with a gentle pull.

If you're dealing with the older, separately mounted taps-and-spout arrangement and have found replacements, start removing the old ones by taking off the tap handles. Pry up the center button and unscrew the retaining screw. Next tap upward lightly on the bottoms of the tap handles until they can be pulled off. Then unscrew the nut or knurled washer that holds the decorative cover over the works of the tap. These taps are inserted up through the holes in the sink and then mounted with retaining nuts and washers coming down from the top. Loosen these nuts, unscrew the spout, and the unit will drop down loose as soon as the lead-in tubes are loosened and taken off the lead-in shut-off valves.

To install new tap spouts you generally reverse the removal procedure. Take a palm-sized gob of plumber's putty from the small can you bought for just such an occasion, and knead it awhile to make it more pliable. Press the putty onto the bottom mounting surface of the unit, then place the unit squarely in position through the holes on the top of the sink. Press the unit down on top of the sink until it rests firmly and squarely. Peel away the excess putty that has been squeezed out and put it back in the can.

From the bottom, run a mounting washer and a retainer nut up onto both threaded taps and tighten the nuts, fixing the unit squarely in place. Insert the stopper-pull rod down through the top and through the mount, and tighten the set screw or bolt. It's usually good practice also to replace the chrome lead-in tubes on these occasions. The ready-cut flexible models work well enough, but don't grab by mistake a pair from the rack holding the ones made for toilet lead-ins. If you're using the old shut-off valves, get two new conically shaped rubber washers and the brass washers that are sandwiched between the rubber and the fastening nut.

Bend the tubes, if need be, so that the ends will enter the shut-off valves and the bottoms of the taps straight. Then cut the tubes to length so that both ends will enter into the threaded fittings at least 1". Now before actually inserting the ends of the tubes into the fittings, place the fastening nuts and washers onto the tubes in the following order at each end: fastening nut, with threaded opening toward the tube end; brass washer; rubber sealing washers with the small end toward the tube end. Pipe compound isn't needed, because the seal is made when the conical washer is pressed into place between the tube and the threaded fitting.

Insert the tube ends into the threaded fittings and run the fastening nuts onto the threads. The trick here is to tighten the nuts far enough to assure a good nonleaking seal at the joint but not so far that the nut will turn the brass washer and rip up the rubber sealer. So run the nuts on finger-tight, then try about one-half turn with the wrench. Don't forget the specialized wrench that is available if you can't quite reach the top fastener nut. You can tighten them farther if they leak when tested.

Test for leaks by turning on the lead-in valve and then turning the taps full on and then off rapidly for a while. Look carefully for pinhole leaks that are hard to spot at first. You can sometimes catch one by feeling all around the tubes for a tiny jet of water. These are annoying, but they sometimes appear because of a flaw in the tubing and the only remedy is a new tube. If there is any dripping from around the bottom end of the tube, test to see whether it isn't actually coming from higher up the tube by checking the tube for runs of water before tightening the bottom fastener nut. The nut just might not be the source of the leak, and another turn may rip up its washer.

Drains are somewhat easier to deal with because of the lower, gravity-fed pressure involved. Most of the drain joints are self-explanatory affairs. Just the same, it might be a good idea to lay the old system out in line as you remove it (with a monkey wrench, pipe wrench or channel lock pliers), so you can see what new parts are needed and in what sequence they should be replaced. Any parts that are pitted around the joints may not have leaked before removal, but they probably will on replacement and should be thrown away.

To remove the actual drainpipe attached to the drain hole in the sink, the usual procedure is to unscrew the stopper raising lever from the back of the drain, remove the stopper from the top of the drain, and then unscrew the stopper lever-holding pipe from the pipe attached to the bottom of the sink. Finally, loosen the large nut against the bottom of the sink and lift out the drain.

Drain fittings not only telescope inside each other at some joints, but also can be bought in varying lengths so that without moving the position of the drain fitting in the wall, you can raise or lower the mounting of a sink or move it to either side with very little trouble. This should be kept in mind when laying out a countertop area. When refitting a drain, try to use new rubber washer rings where needed; and if you need a new part anywhere along the line, take the old one with you when you go to get a new one. Sizes can be deceiving. Also remember that if the pipes are going to be hidden brass is cheaper than chrome-plated brass pipes.

To fit a new drain to a sink, start with the "givens" first, and then move to the more flexible joints. Beginning at the sink drain, check that the sink surfaces around the drain hole in the basin, as well as on the bottom side of the sink, are free from cracks and blemishes. If they can't be smoothed off with a file, use plumber's putty to seal any potential drips. Drop the drainpipe down into the drain hole; run the wide rubber washer onto the bottom of the pipe, then the metal or nylon washer; finally add the retaining nut and tighten it well. Run the female threads of the stopper lever-holding tube onto the threads at the bottom end of the drain, being careful not to get these fine threads cross-threaded. Tighten this joint so that the stopper lever hole is directly at the back of the tube (if you're not using a stopper pulling knob, simply use the plain tube available with the same threading).

Drop the stopper into the drain hole in the basin, and then insert the stopper lever into the hole in the back of the drain tube and tighten the retaining nut. Insert the assembled stopper pull rod down through the hole just behind the spout and through the mount on the lever and tighten the retainer.

Now take the J-shaped pipe that leads the drain into the hole in the wall and slip the retaining nut that sits against its lip at the bottom end of the J onto the pipe, threads first. Next slip on the other retaining nut that attaches the pipe to the wall, threads first, and then the rubber sealing washer. Insert this pipe into the wall and run the fastening nut on finger-tight.

Slip the fastening nut up onto the drain coming out of the sink, threads down, and then slip on the rubber washer. Now attach the U-shaped trap to the end of the drain leading to the wall, as well as the drain coming from the basin. With the joints still only finger-tight, you can pull and turn the various components until the joints are aligned and the retaining nuts can be run onto the threads of the U trap.

Never try to skip this trap fitting with a simplified straight drain arrangement, because the trap is made to catch more than just an occasional diamond ring. The function of the trap is to retain a bit of water which fills the tube across the bottom of the U and blocks odors from coming back up from the sewer and into your sink. Test the drain by running both taps full on and watching for drips.

Removing or Moving a Sink

The great majority of bathroom sinks used in mass-built houses of the past few decades are of the wall-hung ilk. There are older models which bolt directly through the sink into the wall; however, most wall-hangers are mounted on iron holders which hook onto tabs built onto the back sides of the sink. Once the plumbing has been disconnected (see above), the sink can be removed by lifting up on the front of it to break any caulking seal around the back edging, and then lifting the sink out of the mount.

If you plan to move the mount, use a level to mark the new top line for the mount; then hold the mount in the new location and mark the positions of the screw holes on the wall. If you're moving the mount on a tile surface, the old holes can often be covered with stick-on aluminum, stainless steel or copper tiles. Try to find the position of the 2" x 4" framing studs (centered 16" apart) in the wall before settling on a definite lateral position for the mount. The long screws attaching the mount to the wall must bite into something more solid than plaster or drywall, of course. Even expanding-head bolts won't do the trick. When mounting to tile, make marks for the mounting screws with a center punch. Then drill through with a 1/4" masonry bit, being careful not to drill too far into the wood behind the tile.

Sinks already mounted on countertops can be removed by loosening the mounting brackets which hold the sink in place from below.

Removing, Installing and Modifying Toilets

Removing: Start by shutting off the water supply and flushing out the tank. If the lead-in shut-off valve under the tank is in suitable shape, simply shut off the water there. If it shows hints of potential leaks, this may be a good opportunity to replace it. To do this, shut off the water pressure at the meter valve where the water line enters the house. It's a good idea to know just where this valve is anyway, in case of some trick of fate while playing with the pipes.

Whenever dealing with old pipes, the crucial thing to bear in mind is that you don't want to disturb them any more than you have to. When removing the shut-off valve for the toilet, for instance, make certain, before trying to loosen the fitting, that you have a good grip with a wrench on the pipe to which the valve is attached. This way you can keep any twist from being transferred down the line; otherwise, all sorts of nasty things can happen down inside a wall where you can't get at them.

Remove the fastening nut attaching the lead-in tube to the shut-off valve. Remove the valve if it needs replacing and apply pipe joint compound to the threads of the lead-in pipe. Then attach the new valve, being careful once again to hold the lead-in pipe tightly before applying twist to the valve.

203

To remove the tank (if the toilet has a separate tank), loosen the nuts holding the tank bottom against the top rear of the bowl and lift off the tank.

To remove the bowl, pry the mounting bolt covers off the top of the floor mount and loosen the mounting bolts. Slide the bottoms of the bolts along in their grooves in the floor mount until the bottom ends reach the removal hole and can be pulled free. The bowl can then be removed and the wax sealer ring washer carefully cleaned off the top of the drainpipe fitting.

Installing Toilets

To install a toilet the process is generally reversed. Read the instructions on the wax sealer ring and place it right side up, squarely over the drainpipe fitting. Place the bowl carefully in position over the pipe and the ring, and then push down with as little side twisting as possible until the bottom of the bowl mount sits squarely on the floor. Insert the mounting bolts, head down, through the holes in the bowl mount and then down through the removal holes at the ends of the slots in the steel floor mount. Pull the bolts up straight and tighten them. Fix the cover caps over the bolts with epoxy glue or a small tube of car body putty.

If the toilet has a separate tank, insert the two tank mount bolts through the gasket washers provided, then through the mounting holes in the bottom of the tank. Run washers onto the other ends of these bolts, and then secure them tightly against the bottom of the tank with the nuts provided. Place the nylon washer over the water outlet in the center of the tank bottom and then slip on the conical rubber sealer ring, point down, around the outlet. Place the tank on the bowl in position with the water outlet inserted into the large mounting hole in the top rear of the toilet. Then run washers and nuts onto the ends of the mounting bolts and tighten these until the tank sits squarely on the bowl without being able to rock back and forth.

Modifying a Toilet

If a removable shelf is to be mounted on a panel (to hide the tank), a push-button control flush valve may be wanted in order to bring the control out through the front of the panel. Remove the old trip lever by unscrewing the retaining nut inside the tank and unhooking the valve chain. Mount the front of the push-button unit to the front of the lever hole and then attach it to the inside with a fastening nut and hook up the pull chain.

Cut the new lead-in tube so that both ends will extend into the threaded fittings at the shut-off valve and at the bottom of the tank to a depth of about 1". Slip the fastening ring nuts onto the tube, with the threads toward the ends. Then put on the brass washers and the conical rubber sealing washers with the small ends toward the ends of the tubes. Bend the tube so that it enters the threaded fittings squarely and then tighten the fastening nuts enough to prevent leakage but not so tightly that the rubber sealers will be turned and ripped.

204

Check that the float valve can fall easily onto the seating ring around the water outlet. Turn on the water and check for leaks. Pinhole leaks can be felt easier than they can be seen in many cases. If there is a pinhole leak in a tube, due to a defect, replace it. Dripping around the bottom fastener nut can mean either a leak at that fitting or a leak farther up the line. Check for water running down the tubing before further tightening the bottom fastener nut.

If the water in the tank fills to above the water level line indicated on the inside of the tank, bend the arm holding the float down. Or, with sliding floats, lengthen the rod-length adjustment connecting the float to the valve arm. If the level is too low, bend the float arm up or shorten the rod length for sliding floats.

Now test the flushing action and the flush valve for leaks by listening carefully for the sound of a trickle leak which continues long after the tank refilling has stopped. Small adjustments on the alignment of the flush valve on the seating can usually cure this after a few tries.

Index

The Authors

Necessity is the mother of most do-it-yourselfers, and so it was for the Stevensons when they were first faced with the problem of living in an "unbelievably unimaginative" house. Blessed with a taste for better things and an almost non-existent budget, they decided to invest what little they could venture into raw materials and plunge into the rebuilding jobs themselves, learning to do the labor as they went along.

After running into nearly every possible pitfall, the Stevensons slowly came to grips with the practice of giving an original, personal appeal to houses without using highly skilled professional techniques. And it seems to have paid off, both visually and economically.

Six renovated houses later, they come to us with their book—the book they say they would have given anything for when they first started trying to do the jobs needed to make a house a better place to live.

They now live in Del Mar, California with their son, Mike, and their daughter, Shannon, and an overbearing cat named Claude.